RISKS & REWARDS
Of Entrepreneurship

by
M. Catherine Ashmore
Lisa Mazzei Fischer
Gwendolyn Rippey
Terry W. Southwick
Laurel A. Zlotnick
Frieda Douthitt

The National Center
for Research in Vocational Education
The Ohio State University
Columbus, Ohio

Changing Times Education Service
EMC Publishing
Saint Paul, Minnesota

The development of this product was sponsored by
The Ohio Department of Education,
Division of Vocational and Career Education

Design, Photography, Production
Slater Studio, Minneapolis, MN

Library of Congress Catalog Number: 87-21787

ISBN 0-8219-0323-3

© 1988 by The National Center for Research in
Vocational Education, The Ohio State University

All rights reserved. No part of this publication can be adapted,
reproduced, stored in a retrieval system or transmitted in any
form or by any means, electronic, mechanical, photocopying,
recording, or otherwise without permission from the publisher.

Published by EMC Publishing
300 York Avenue
St. Paul, Minnesota 55101

Printed in the United States of America
0 9 8 7 6 5 4

Dear Student:

As you complete your high school years, are you experiencing any of these feelings?

- Pressured to choose a career
- Overwhelmed by all the choices you see before you
- Afraid of being on your own
- Scared that you will not find a job
- Afraid of the responsibilities you will have

Many people make decisions about their future without careful thought and consideration. Although poor decisions can be learning experiences, much needless suffering can be avoided by carefully examining your choices before making a decision. If you think about it, you are likely to spend more time on your job than any area of your life. Therefore, it is important to make your career decision as wisely as you can.

In this book, you will learn about becoming an entrepreneur as a possible career choice. An entrepreneur is one who organizes, manages, and assumes the risks of a business. By exploring entrepreneurship or small business ownership as a career option, you will expand your choices and learn more about your own abilities.

So let's look at information about you and your business ideas, which will help you explore entrepreneurship as well as other career alternatives. Even if you decide that entrepreneurship isn't for you after you complete this book, you will know yourself and your career needs better.

Throughout the book you will complete activities which are labeled Profile #___. By completing them and saving them for future reference, you will have an excellent file of personal information to use in job interviews, investor interviews, self-development, and competitive events, or to help you start your own business.

Best of luck!

Table of Contents

Section 1

Can I Be an Entrepreneur?....................................1

What Do You Know about Yourself?......................................2
Personal Profile 1   Personal Characteristics Assessment..............3
What Do We Know about Entrepreneurs?..................................4
How Are You Like Entrepreneurs?.......................................5
Personal Profile 2   Characterists: Assets and Potential..............5
How Does Entrepreneurship Affect Life-style?..........................6
What Are Your Life-style Preferences?.................................7
Personal Profile 3   Life-style Preference Classification.............7
Are Your Preferences Compatible with Becoming an Entrepreneur?........8
How Can Entrepreneurial Career Planning Help You?....................10
Did You Know?..10
Do You Know Yourself Better than Before?.............................11
Activities...11
Success Stories..20
The Think Tank...27

Section 2

What Experiences Have I Had?....................................28

What Is Experience?..29
What Types of Aptitudes Might You Have?..............................30
Personal Profile 4   Experience and Aptitudes........................31
Personal Profile 5   Aptitudes Worksheet.............................32
What Are Your Interests?...32
Personal Profile 6   Experience — Interests.........................33
Personal Profile 7   Interests Grouped According to Similarities.....34
What Knowledge Is Important to an Entrepreneur?......................34
What Skills Will I Need as an Entrepreneur?..........................35
Personal Profile 8   Your Experiences Develop Skills.................37
How Does an Entrepreneur Gain Expertise?.............................38
Are You Building Career Expertise?...................................38
Activities...39
Success Stories..48
The Think Tank...55

Section 3
What Type of Business Could I Start? 56

What Is a Business Idea? 57
Where Do You Get Your Business Idea? 58
What Business Ideas Can You Think of Related to Using Your Vocational
    Training? 60
Personal Profile 9   Businesses Based on Your Vocational Experience 61
How Can Interests, Skills, and Hobbies Lead to a Business Idea? 62
Personal Profile 10   Businesses Based on Your Interests, Skills,
    and Hobbies 63
What Business Might You Start Someday? 64
Personal Profile 11   My Business 64
Why Should You Know about Your Community? 66
How Large Is Your Community? 66
Why Should You Know about the People? 66
Why Should You Know about Competition? 67
Why Should You Know about Changes in Your Community? 68
Personal Profile 12   Market Area Changes 68
Why Should You Know about Foreign Business? 70
What Sort of Business Might You Start Someday? 70
Activities 71
Success Stories 81
The Think Tank 88

Section 4
How Can I Prepare to Be My Own Boss? 89

How Do Entrepreneurs View Risk? 90
Is Becoming an Entrepreneur too Risky? 91
Why Worry about Decisions? 91
How Do You Make Your Decisions? 92
Personal Profile 13   Career Decision-Making Steps 93
Why Are Goals Important? 94
How Do You Reach Your Goals? 95
Personal Profile 14   Setting Personal Goals 96
Why Should You Begin to Build Resources? 98
What Types of Resources Should You Begin to Build? 99
Who Are the Contacts? 99
Personal Profile 15   Contact/Resource List 101
What Do You Need to be Prepared to Do? 102
Where Can an Entrepreneur Go for Assistance? 102
Activities 102
Success Stories 112
The Think Tank 119
Glossary 120

Section 1

Can I Be an Entrepreneur?

Completing this section will help you—

- ★ assess personal characteristics
- ★ identify how entrepreneurship affects life-style
- ★ evaluate life-style preferences
- ★ recognize the importance of career planning

"Minds are like parachutes—
they work only when open."

Anonymous

What Is This Section About?

When you woke up this morning and looked into the mirror, what did you see? You probably saw your reflection just as you had seen yourself thousands of other mornings. But that face belongs to a special person—you. You are one of a kind! Others may be similar, but you have your own unique set of characteristics and talents. You may be mechanically talented while your friend is artistically talented. You prefer vanilla ice cream and your friend prefers chocolate.

Through the exercises in this section you will examine your personal characteristics and life-style preferences. As you learn more about yourself, you will be able to make better career choices.

You also will learn about some of the personal characteristics and life-style preferences of entrepreneurs so that you can compare them to yours. The comparison will give you a clearer picture of your compatibility with entrepreneurship at this stage of your life. Even if you find that you are not interested in entrepreneurship now, you will improve your self-understanding.

What Do You Know about Yourself?

Because you have lived with yourself every moment since birth, you probably think you know yourself completely. But unless you pay close attention to all your feelings and behaviors, you probably don't notice many of them. Although it is impossible to know yourself completely, the following activity will help you examine some of your personal characteristics.

Can I Be an Entrepreneur?

Personal Profile 1

Personal Characteristics Assessment

Instructions: This assessment will help you compare your personal characteristics to the characteristics that entrepreneurs tend to exhibit. Put an X under the response you feel best describes you. Answer the questions honestly. There are no wrong answers, so you will not be graded on your responses.

	Rarely or No	Mostly or Yes
1. Do you like taking chances?	_____	_____
2. Do you like school?	_____	_____
3. Do you like making your own decisions on the job?	_____	_____
4. Do you get bored easily?	_____	_____
5. Do you sleep as little as possible?	_____	_____
6. Do you feel unexpected energy when you tackle things that you like?	_____	_____
7. Do you finish what you start?	_____	_____
8. Do you take risks for the thrill of it?	_____	_____
9. Do you plan your tasks before getting started?	_____	_____
10. Do you worry about what others think of you?	_____	_____
11. Do you find it easy to get others to do something for you?	_____	_____
12. Do you enjoy doing something just to prove you can do it?	_____	_____
13. Do you find yourself constantly thinking up new ideas?	_____	_____
14. Do you like to take care of details?	_____	_____
15. Do you believe there should be security in a job?	_____	_____

What Do We Know about Entrepreneurs?

There is no absolute definition of what you have to be like to be an entrepreneur. However, certain personality characteristics are commonly seen in people who start a business. Some of these personal characteristics usually found in entrepreneurs are presented here.

- ★ **Risk taking.** To chance the possibility of loss. To some, risk taking seems foolish and dangerous, but many entrepreneurs see it as an adventure because they believe in their own abilities to succeed.

- ★ **Learning-oriented.** To gain skill through experience. Closely related to risk taking, learning often requires making mistakes. Entrepreneurs view this as necessary for improvement.

- ★ **Independent.** To be free to choose one's own actions. Entrepreneurs want to make their own decisions about how to run their businesses.

- ★ **Responsible.** To be answerable for one's conduct and obligations. Entrepreneurs hold themselves accountable for their own decisions and actions.

- ★ **Impatient.** To become restless when delayed. Entrepreneurs prefer quick actions and results because they have high energy levels.

- ★ **Efficient.** To be productive without waste. Due to the heavy demands of operating their own business, entrepreneurs maximize every waking moment.

- ★ **Resourceful.** To meet the demands of unexpected situations. Entrepreneurs are creative problem solvers.

- ★ **Determined.** To continue trying until the problem is solved. Entrepreneurs do not give up when faced with a problem. They search for a way to overcome problems.

- ★ **Goal-oriented.** To aim your efforts toward a desired end. Entrepreneurs decide what they want, plan to achieve it, and make the plan work.

- ★ **Self-confident.** To see yourself as talented and able. Entrepreneurs believe in their abilities to succeed.

- ★ **Leaders.** To direct and manage activities. Strong direction and decision making are characteristic of entrepreneurs' leadership.

- ★ **Creative.** To design or make something new. Entrepreneurs are always on the lookout for new and better ways to do things.

Entrepreneurs were not born with these characteristics. They developed them through experience. It is possible that you too will develop these characteristics through your experiences if you haven't already.

How Are You Like Entrepreneurs?

Now that you have reviewed some entrepreneurial characteristics, compare your Personal Characteristics Assessment to the Entrepreneur's Response Key at the end of the book. (As you compare, remember that having few matches doesn't mean that you aren't suited to own your own business.)

If you decide to become an entrepreneur in the future, you simply need to develop some of the characteristics that you are lacking. Complete the following activity to determine the characteristics that you may need to develop.

Personal Profile 2

Characteristics: Assets and Potential

Instructions: Now that you have a better understanding of some entrepreneurial characteristics, answer the following questions to see how you compare to a typical entrepreneur and to determine characteristics you may wish to develop.

1. Which entrepreneurial characteristics do you have?

2. What could you do to develop the characteristics you are missing?

Now you have a glimpse of yourself in relation to owning your own business. This assessment measured only one aspect of you (your personal characteristics). You will evaluate life-style preferences next to obtain a more thorough self-understanding.

How Does Entrepreneurship Affect Life-style?

Your values are self-guiding principles for your life. Values shape your life-style. Small business ownership may make demands on your life-style that lead to a values conflict. A values conflict occurs when you act in a way that you don't believe is correct.

For example, most entrepreneurs work 50–70 hours per week. Perhaps you do not want to work more than 40 hours a week. If you become an entrepreneur and work 50–70 hours per week, you probably will feel out of touch with yourself and wonder why life doesn't seem as meaningful to you as it once did. If you work only 40 hours per week, your business may fail. This is a values conflict.

Or maybe you feel strongly that Sunday is a day to be spent at home with your family. In order to reach some of your customers, your business may have to be open on Sunday. This will require you to work and be away from your family, causing a values conflict.

Failure to examine your life-style preferences (values) before becoming an entrepreneur could lead to serious values conflicts. A closer look at life-style preferences will help you to avoid this pitfall.

What Are Your Life-style Preferences?

During a typical day, you make many choices about the activities you will do according to your values. The activities you would like to do are your life-style preferences. You don't always do the activities that you prefer because you have needs that must be met.

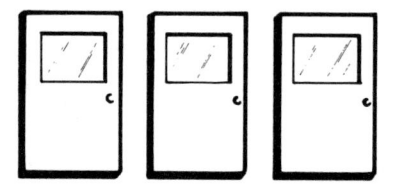

For example, you may not wish to work at all. But since work is necessary for your basic survival needs, such as food and shelter, you will work. Consequently, the challenge is to achieve a balance between your needs and preferences.

Many times this balancing is done without much thought. Since it is unlikely that you will be able to fulfill all of your preferences, carefully consider the importance of each one while doing the next activity.

Personal Profile 3

Life-style Preference Classification

Instructions: A quick way to determine your life-style preferences is to rank them. Read through the list and, starting with your most important value, rank them from 1 to 10, with 1 being the most important and 10 being the least important. Please give this activity serious thought. Be careful to rate the preferences according to what you want, not by what others want you to do.

_____ Personal hobbies	_____ Taking vacations
_____ Being creative	_____ Evenings at home with family
_____ Job security	_____ Watching TV
_____ Time with friends	_____ Being the boss
_____ Challenging career	_____ Sense of accomplishment

Instructions: Name and explain how at least one of your life-style preferences would be complementary to entrepreneurship as your future career.

Instructions: Name and discuss in writing at least one life-style preference you have that may cause a conflict if you become an entrepreneur. Discuss whether or not you think the conflict would be worth the trade-off.

Are Your Preferences Compatible with Becoming an Entrepreneur?

For you to find satisfaction as an entrepreneur, there must be a match between the demands of entrepreneurship and your life-style preferences. Being the boss, feeling a sense of accomplishment, being creative, and having a challenging career are preferences that are highly associated with entrepreneurs. If you choose to become an entrepreneur, these preferences will often require you to sacrifice vacations, evenings at home with the family, watching TV, and many other leisure activities.

You may find preferences that can be complementary to owning your own business, such as turning your cooking hobby into a catering business or working out of the home to be with your children. Another option would be to start your business on a part-time basis until you begin to make enough money to support yourself. You could then quit your other job and devote all your energy to building a successful business.

As mentioned earlier, you may find some values conflicts. Remember, the deciding factor is the importance of the preferences to you. For example, if you ranked job security as most important (#1), running your own business would cause a values conflict since there are no guarantees and the risk is great. In contrast, if you ranked job security as #5 after sense of accomplishment, being the boss, challenging career, and being creative, you would fulfill your most important preferences by becoming an entrepreneur.

The compatibility of your preferences with entrepreneurship may not be so clear-cut. You may have conflicting preferences that you consider equally important, such as being the boss and spending evenings at home with family. In such situations, it is helpful to examine your other preferences to clarify the best choice.

Whatever the results of your examination today, your life-style preferences may change many times throughout your life as you gain new experiences and opportunities.

How Can Entrepreneurial Career Planning Help You?

Career plans are simply road maps for our lives which guide us to the destination we want to reach. Living without career plans is like setting out on an ocean voyage without a compass. Just as the likelihood of reaching the planned port in this case is doubtful, life without career plans is likely to leave you beached on unknown shores. Career plans help you limit your actions to activities that will help you achieve your desires. The approximately 1 in 19 Americans who excels has done so because of planning.

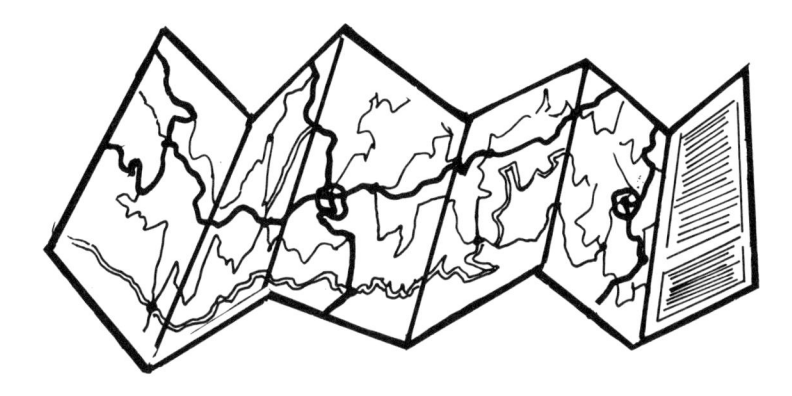

The best career plans are based on self-knowledge and desires. Hopefully, self-examination of your personal characteristics and life-style values has brought you a bit closer to setting a career plan. In the next unit you will explore your knowledge, skills, and experiences, which will further enhance your self-knowledge.

Did You Know?

Small business creators come in all kinds of sizes and shapes. No one can predict who will or won't make it work. Researchers have tried to find some common element for entrepreneurs that students may match. A recent report on entrepreneurs from the National Federation of Independent Business suggests the following:

- About 40 percent of entrepreneurs had a high school degree or less.

- About 50 percent of entrepreneurs had parents who owned a business.

- Thirty-five percent of entrepreneurs were under the age of 30.

- Entrepreneurs generally believe they can control their own future.

- It is psychologically easier to start a business when you are around others who are doing it.

- Job experience acts as an incubator for employees who are getting ready to branch into their own business.

- More than 50 percent of entrepreneurs start businesses in the areas in which they already have job experience.

- Personal savings are the most important source of funds to the beginning entrepreneur.

- Most people start businesses where they are already living and working.

- Qualities such as determination, energy, and an ability to learn from previous experience can make a difference.

- Successful entrepreneurs tend to seek advice from outside professionals.

- Success does not mean the same to all entrepreneurs.

- Entrepreneurs are influenced early in their lives by people like themselves who are already successful in business (role models).

- Due to the baby boom generation, there are more persons with credentials and fewer challenging jobs in today's job market.

- Some 87 percent of new jobs are created by small business.

- More and more people will change careers at least once in their lifetime.

Do You Know Yourself Better than Before?

In this section you discovered your own uniqueness. You examined your personal characteristics and learned about those of an entrepreneur. However, there is no absolute definition of what characteristics an entrepreneur possesses. An entrepreneur is not born with certain characteristics; he or she develops these certain characteristics through experiences. You read that being an entrepreneur can affect a person's life-style. Hopefully, you now have a better idea of some life-style preferences that are important to you and have thought about how they may be complementary to owning your own business. Knowing yourself will aid you in developing career plans.

Activities

The following activities are designed to help you develop a better self-awareness of your entrepreneurial potential. Complete the activities assigned by your instructor as thoughtfully as possible. Some of the activities will give you added insights into your life-style preferences. One activity will provide you with a firsthand knowledge of what life is like as an entrepreneur.

Can I Be an Entrepreneur?

Crossword Puzzle

Instructions: This activity will help you review the terms you learned in this section. Read the clues and then fill in the puzzle.

Across

1. People who develop an idea into a business, assuming the risks involved. Also includes managing, organizing, and planning this new enterprise.
2. Choices made by weighing the costs of preferences and determining whether one is able to pay the price.
3. An entrepreneurial characteristic of developing ideas.
4. Acquiring knowledge through experiences and the desire to know more.
5. Due to the _____ _____ (two words) generation, there are more persons with credentials and fewer challenging jobs in today's job market.
6. Self-guiding principles in one's life.
7. Approximately one in _____ Americans who excels does so because he or she has career plans.
8. A characteristic of an entrepreneur that shows an inability or lack of desire for waiting. Entrepreneurs usually prefer quick action.

Down

9. Entrepreneurial characteristic where the entrepreneur is accountable for his or her decisions. This trait works closely with that of independence.
10. More than ever before people are changing _____ at least once.
11. Often the way people live their lives is an expression of values (definition).
12. Entrepreneurial characteristic where one takes a chance that could result in financial loss or gain. Many entrepreneurs consider this ability challenging and adventurous due to confidence in themselves.
13. These function as a road map to guide people's lives to a destination they want to reach.
14. Forty percent of entrepreneurs have a _____ _____ (two words) education or less.
15. People will most likely spend more time on their _____ than any area of their life.
16. An entrepreneurial trait demonstrated by maximizing every possible waking moment because of the excessive demands of operating one's own business.
17. A characteristic of entrepreneurs that shows they do not want to rely on someone else; they want to control their own environment.
18. An entrepreneurial characteristic marked by quick action and vigor. Entrepreneurs do not seem to tire easily.

Can I Be an Entrepreneur?

13

Starting Your Own Business— A Quick Self-Assessment Checklist

You want to own and manage your own business. It is a good idea–provided you know what it takes and have what it takes. Starting a business is risky at best, but your chances of making it increase if you understand the problems you will meet and work to solve as many of them as you can before you start.

Here are some questions to help you think through what you need to know and do. Under each question, check the answer that says what you feel, or comes closest to it. Be honest with yourself.

Are you a self-starter?

_____ I do things on my own. Nobody has to tell me to get going.

_____ If someone gets me started, I keep going all right.

_____ Easy does it. I do not put myself out until I have to.

How do you feel about other people?

_____ I like people. I can get along with just about everybody.

_____ I have plenty of friends. I do not need anyone else.

_____ Most people irritate me.

Can you lead others?

_____ I can get most people to go along when I start something.

_____ I can give orders if someone tells me what we should do.

_____ I let someone else get things moving, then I go along if I feel like it.

Can you take responsibility?

_____ I like to take charge of things and see them through.

_____ I will take over if I have to, but I would rather let someone else be responsible.

_____ There is always some eager beaver around wanting to show how smart he or she is. I say let him or her.

How good a worker are you?

_____ I can keep going as long as I need to. I do not mind working hard for something I want.

_____ I will work hard for awhile, but when I have had enough, that is it.

_____ I cannot see that hard work gets you anywhere.

Continued on Next Page

Can you make decisions comfortably?

_____ I can make up my mind in a hurry if I have to. It usually turns out OK, too.

_____ I can make up my mind if I have plenty of time. If I have to make decisions quickly, I think later that it should have been decided another way.

_____ I do not like to be the one who has to decide things.

Can people trust what you say?

_____ You bet they can. I do not say things I do not mean.

_____ I try to be on the level most of the time, but sometimes I just say what is easiest.

_____ Why bother if the other fellow does not know the difference?

Can you stick with it?

_____ If I make up my mind to do something, I do not let anything stop me.

_____ I usually finish what I start–if it goes well.

_____ If things do not go right from the start, I quit. Why beat your brains out?

How good is your health?

_____ I never run down.

_____ I have enough energy for most of the things I want to do.

_____ I run out of energy sooner, it seems, than most of my friends.

Now count the checks you have made. How many checks are there beside the first answer to each question? the second answer to each question? the third answer to each question?

If most of your checks are beside the first answer, you probably have what it takes to run a business. If not, you are likely to have more trouble than you can handle by yourself. Better find a partner who is strong on the points in which you are weak. If many checks are beside the third answer, not even a good business partner will be able to shore you up.

Source: Adapted from *Occupational Quarterly*, Winter 1979, SBA Management Aids No. 171, as it appears in American Association of Community and Junior Colleges, *Small Business Course for Older Americans*, Instructor's Guide (Washington, DC, AACJC).

Entrepreneur Interview Questions

Instructions: Arrange to interview an entrepreneur and use this list of questions to ask during an interview with him or her. Write a case study about him or her based on the responses. Use the "Success Stories" found in this book as a guideline for your own case study. (Your local Small Business Administration office and chamber of commerce are good sources for names if you don't know any entrepreneurs.)

1. When did you first decide that you wanted to work for yourself?

2. What were your career plans when you graduated from high school?

3. How many hours do you work a week?

4. Do you enjoy doing something just to prove you can?

5. Do you believe there should be security in a job?

6. Do you plan your tasks before getting started?

7. What are your hobbies?

8. How much time do you spend watching TV?

9. How much time do you spend with friends and family?

10. What do you like about having your own business?

Continued on Next Page

11. What do you dislike about having your own business?

12. What have been the most severe conflicts that you have had with your life-style since starting your own business?

13. How did you deal with these conflicts?

14. Do you feel that owning your own business has been worth the conflicts that you have had to deal with?

Case Study

Life-style Choices

You have just accepted a job promotion. You are being transferred to a small island in the South Pacific. Due to government restrictions on the island, you may only take three persons or possessions with you. Possible choices may include pet, family member, friend, life savings, stereo, television, car, stationery and pen, camera, book, newspaper, or any others you can think of. List your three choices.

Are the life-style preferences that your choices indicate compatible with entrepreneurship? Why or why not?

Life-style Decisions

Imagine that the doctor has just told you that you have only 5 years left to live. List the things you would like to do before time runs out.

Does this give you a different picture of yourself and your desires? Hopefully, you will have uncovered your most important life-style preferences. Take one preference and write a plan to accomplish it.

Can I Be an Entrepreneur?

Success Stories

Read these success stories carefully and then answer the questions. Each of the entrepreneurs you will read about graduated from a vocational program. Think about what characteristics make each one unique and led to his or her starting a business? Perhaps you will find one who has characteristics and life-style preferences similar to yours.

Name: Brett Gibson

Business Name: Mid-American Telephone Supply

Business Address: 4575 Wabash Avenue
Terre Haute, IN 47803

Business Phone: (812) 877-2442

Type of Business: Telephone systems and equipment sales, installation and service

Brett Gibson, while possibly not unique, certainly is an unusual person. At the age of 10 he started his own business as a hobby, selling and installing telephones. He was mostly self-taught, although a fifth-grade teacher had gotten him interested in electronics, which was to become valuable as his business diversified.

His business grew steadily until, at the ripe old age of 15, Brett decided to expand into commercial telephone systems as well. About that time, Terre Haute enacted an ordinance requiring licensing of all telephone installers, and Brett was to become fully acquainted with age discrimination. Included in that ordinance were the requirements that licensed installers be at least 18 years of age and have five years of experience.

Brett says, "I have never given up when told I could not do something." He applied for his license and was turned down by the city controller because he was too young. He went through "the longest battle of my life." Brett was still doing battle when a local newspaper intervened on his behalf. At last the age restriction was removed. (The experience restriction may soon be lowered also, although it does not affect Brett.)

Brett sees himself as a determined, innovative go-getter, and the success of his business seems to bear this out. His company now has over 250 commercial telephone systems in service, some in large corporations. He employs seven full-time people.

While Brett has learned the business mainly on his own, he has had help from telephone distributors across the country with such things as growth, setting up accounts, and establishing credit. His parents, too, have given him a lot of support. The local Chamber of Commerce has been helpful by providing Brett with advice on setting up and advertising his new location.

Continued on Next Page

Today, at 17, Brett is a senior in the marketing education program at North Vigo High School. Here he is learning the language of business and some all-important administrative skills. "I feel that DECA [Distributive Education Clubs of America] is teaching me even more business terms and is getting me involved with the standard business practices."

Brett is proud that in a field with a high failure rate he is succeeding. "I feel the most creative aspect of my business involves the complexity of the communications industry. Most interconnect companies in the area can't keep up." He targets businesses that rent their phone systems and are dissatisfied with the service they are receiving. These people are "still paying the high prices of renting...when they could purchase the system and pay it off in one or two years." Mid-American's territory at present includes Indiana and all surrounding states.

Brett intends to continue his company's growth in the communications field, from business telephone systems to cellular telephone service. "I want to have the only telephone interconnect company in Terre Haute, and I'm very close," says Brett. The company is presently expanding into nationwide distribution of telephone equipment.

Case Study Questions

Brett Gibson
Mid-American Telephone Supply

1. How did Brett find a business niche that he could fill? What community needs does his business serve?

2. What particular kind of discrimination did Brett face, and how did he surmount it?

3. From these experiences, what do you recognize about Brett's character that will help him succeed in business?

4. What school experiences were especially helpful to Brett as an entrepreneur? How has DECA (Distributive Education Clubs of America) been valuable?

5. What goals has Brett set for his business?

. . . .

Name: Robert P. Downs

Business Name: Finite System Programming

Business Address: P.O. Box 483
New Paltz, NY 12561

Business Phone: (914) 255-4400

Type of Business: Computer consulting and programming

Ten years ago a young teen sat in front of a computer fascinated by the mystical powers before him on the screen. From the moment he set his fingers on the keyboard, Robert Downs longed to become a computer programmer.

When Robert was a teenager, his father gave up a secure job and moved his family from Illinois to New Jersey to become a one-third partner in a faltering business left to him by *his* father. His courage and hard work turned the company around.

His example was not lost on Robert, whose motto is "No guts, no glory." The "glory" of succeeding with the computer programming business that he started when he was 19 is, for now, the sense of being his own boss and, for the future, the ability to retire early. Like his father, strong motivation, tempered with humility and honesty, is the key to Robert Downs' success story.

Robert took all the electronics and computer courses he could while in high school. He didn't find out about the computer course at Board of Cooperative Educational Services, Goshen, New York, until his senior year, but he was able to pass competency tests and take a two-year program in one year.

He had already formed his own computer company when he entered the State University of New York at New Paltz, New York. Although his computer programming experience proved to be useful, he also realized the value of business organization and management courses.

Now 23, he wants to graduate, but can only attend college part-time because of the demands of his business, which last year grossed $100,000.

Continued on Next Page

Computer programming, Robert explains, is necessary for anyone who has a lot of data to keep track of and compile statistics on. At the outset, Robert did not do much market research. "I just haphazardly went after something," he admits.

One of his early clients was his own vocational school. He sold them a bank simulation program for banking classes. Then he realized that government has many needs for computer programming and can also pay high prices for it. He now has 11 district attorney's offices as clients. He wrote a program by which district attorneys can keep track of everyone in the state with a drunk driving record.

Now Robert is targeting his services more to the private sector. While the large government contracts still supplement the business, Robert says that they, "can now afford to take more and more private low-cost programming."

In forming his company, Robert had the advantage of thousands of dollars worth of legal services given free by an attorney friend who drew up the necessary documents to protect Robert against theft of his work. On the advice of his accountant, he incorporated, since his company files a lot of copyright patents and a corporation receives more protection under the law.

Robert finds it necessary to subsidize his programming with a hardware division headed by a partner. One of his goals is to narrow the company's focus to programming. His long-range goal is to make the company self-supporting on program royalties and use income from new sales to generate new programs.

Although he works "much much more than 40 hours a week," Robert tries to take frequent vacations. His idea of relaxing is to lie on a beach and think about new projects. Business is never out of his mind as he thinks of new ways to produce "quality products without compromise."

The company is growing fast. It now has five employees and twice last year moved to larger quarters. Robert is realistic about his role in it: "Somebody with my lack of skills can easily bring a company down. I don't belong at the top. I have the guts to start it, but others will run it," he says.

"Half the people I know can out-program me. But if you're not motivated, if you're not driven, I don't think you can succeed. And I have that. I have motivation."

Case Study Questions

Robert P. Downs
Computer Programming

1. "If you want to start your own business, you have to be very, very hungry," Robert Downs recently told a business class. What do you think he meant?

2. What is the key to Robert's success?

3. For Robert, what are the rewards of owning his own business?

4. What is his idea of a vacation?

5. In your opinion, will Robert Downs retire early?

. . . .

Name: Tawaunna L. Jones

Business Name: Senoj Fashions and Cosmetics

Business Address: 200 Rhode Island Ave., NE, Suite 129
Washington, DC 20002

Business Phone: (202) 529-6338

Type of Business: Fashions, cosmetics, and models' workshop

Tawaunna Jones wanted to go to medical school and become a psychiatrist, but in distributive education at H.D. Woodson High School, Washington, DC, she changed her mind.

A skilled seamstress even as a child, Tawaunna began sewing clothes for other people at age 12. She "pinched pennies," she says, to pay for her education. In DECA activities, she began to see that those savings could finance the start of her own fashion business.

Continued on Next Page

Now 27, she is president of Senoj (Jones spelled backwards), a fashion and cosmetic retail business that also trains both male and female models and helps them find jobs.

Tawaunna was a good student, an eager learner. She went on to further schooling after high school, studying fashion design and business management at Virginia Commonwealth University, Richmond, VA. She majored in French and business at USDA Graduate School in Washington, DC, and got further training in fashion design at Paris Fashion Institute, Paris, France, where one of the requirements was to design and fabricate two collections of 100 garments each. She rounded out her education with experience as designer, fabricator, and fitter in major department stores and couturier shops.

Senoj, as she's now known, is invited to exhibit her designs at fashion shows in the nation's capital. Her clothes feature bold lines and fabrics. They are designed to bring high fashion to women who want to dress well on a budget.

The Senoj cosmetic line, which she has manufactured by a cosmetics lab in New York, is especially formulated for problem skins. Her clientele, Tawaunna says, is "ladies who often have a hard time getting waited on at the make-up counter."

Her modeling workshops teach a thorough introduction to the world of fashion modeling to prospective models as young as five.

Tawaunna possesses an extra measure of determination which has helped her overcome the double disadvantage of being a black woman in the business world. "It's twice as hard," she says. "Funding doesn't come easily. But," she says, "we can't run away from prejudice."

She chose the name "Senoj" because "it's sexless and colorless and helps me get through a lot of doors."

"I don't listen to the word, 'no,'" she says. "I believe in trying even if all the odds are against you." She tries to look at failures from the positive side "and figure out the lessons to be learned."

She credits her success to hard work, 12-hour days, "doing what no one else would do," and a motto that forms the acronym LAW: "Look like a woman, Act like a lady, and Work like a dog."

Senoj advises students who think about going into business for themselves to keep a part-time or full-time job at first until the business is going well.

"They must realize that the road will not be easy. They must pay their dues over a period of time. Too often, people give up after five years. Making a success of a business takes longer," she says.

Tawaunna has paid her dues. She worked long days, sacrificing many hours of personal and social life. Now she is reaping rewards that she likes. Not all of them are financial.

"You get more satisfaction when you work for yourself," Tawaunna says. "I dance to my own beat. It depends on me, not on my supervisor's budget for that year."

Case Study Questions

Tawaunna L. Jones
Senoj

1. How did her experience in DECA change Tawaunna Jones' life?

2. In addition to sewing skills, what personal qualities does Tawaunna possess that have helped her succeed?

3. What is Tawaunna's motto? How can such sayings be helpful?

4. What does Tawaunna mean when she says that new entrepreneurs must "pay their dues"?

5. For Tawaunna, what is a suitable trial period for a new business?

The Think Tank

Can I Be an Entrepreneur?

Instructions: Summarize what you have learned in this section by writing your personal responses to these questions as a private journal entry to keep for use in your future career planning.

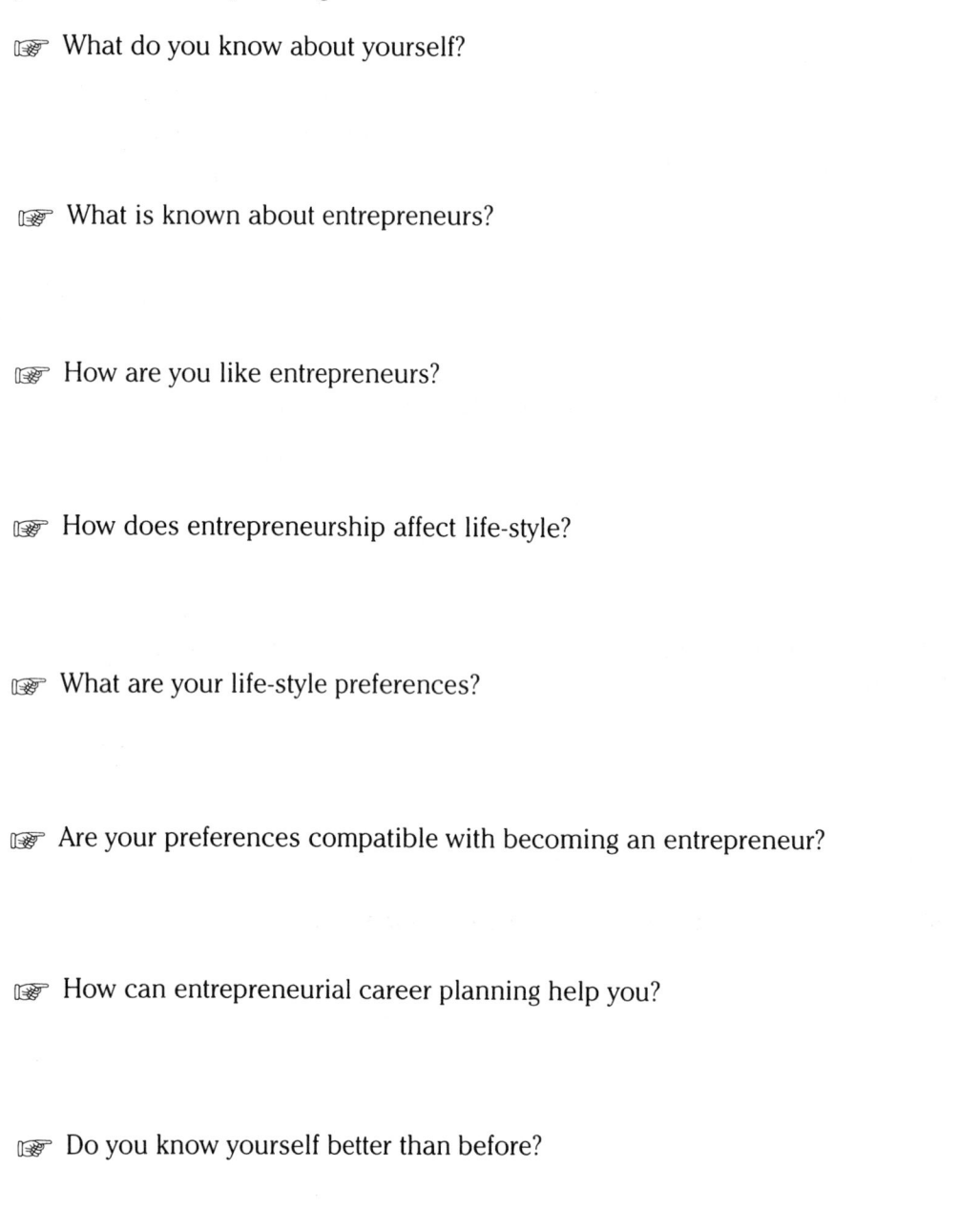

☞ What do you know about yourself?

☞ What is known about entrepreneurs?

☞ How are you like entrepreneurs?

☞ How does entrepreneurship affect life-style?

☞ What are your life-style preferences?

☞ Are your preferences compatible with becoming an entrepreneur?

☞ How can entrepreneurial career planning help you?

☞ Do you know yourself better than before?

Section 2

What Experiences Have I Had?

Completing this section will help you—

- ★ examine past and present experiences
- ★ evaluate aptitudes, interests, knowledge, and skills
- ★ determine current business expertise

"Entrepreneurs are not born; they become through learning and life experiences."

—*Al Shapero*

What Is This Section About?

Before choosing a career goal, it is important to identify your current skills and interests. Evaluation of current skills will enable you to choose career goals that use those skills. Also, it will help to determine where you need to seek additional assistance or experiences.

In this section you will review your own experiences, aptitudes, knowledge, skills, and interests in relation to a career. More specifically, you will compare that information to the expertise entrepreneurs or small business owners often have. Entrepreneurship and/or small business ownership is not for everyone; however, it is an alternative career you will want to explore.

Remember that new experiences and additional education strengthens and develops knowledge. This knowledge and skills may someday help you successfully start and run a business.

What is Experience?

Experiences take place when knowledge (learning) or skills are acquired through watching or being involved in an event. Past experiences help shape future skills and knowledge. Experiences are also related to your background, values, life-style, and personal attributes (section 1). Experiences can include a number of different events. Examples of experiences follow.

- Going to youth camp for a week
- Watching a play
- Attending a class
- Learning a craft, or learning how to play an instrument
- Serving as an officer in VICA, DECA, FFA, FHA/HERO, or OEA
- Doing a community project (community cleanup, visiting a nursing home)
- Receiving an award
- Chairing a committee
- Serving as a member of a committee
- Taking part in family activities
- Receiving your first paycheck

Think about some experiences you have had. Jot some of these down on a piece of paper. You may want to use them later in this section.

What Types of Aptitudes Might You Have?

Aptitudes are natural talents or inclinations for certain activities. People have a broad range of aptitudes. For instance, Karla may have a very high aptitude for artistic activities. She draws and then paints the sets used in the school plays. These activities just seem to come naturally.

At the same time, Karla has very little aptitude in numerical activities. The study of mathematics is very difficult for this student. Often, people will enjoy doing those things in which they have a strong or high aptitude much more than something that takes greater effort. Some examples of aptitudes include the following:

- ★ *Verbal or nonverbal communications* (written or spoken words or actions that communicate ideas, emotions or events). Giving a speech in class, acting in a school play, and hugging a friend are all methods of communication.

- ★ *Verbal comprehension* (understanding the meanings of ideas or emotions in verbal or nonverbal communication). Listening and reacting to a friend's problem, discussing politics, and trying to sell neighbors on your abilities to mow their lawns are examples of verbal comprehension.

- ★ *Logical* (applying reason or logic to problems). Solving a math problem or measuring the fabric available and deciding if there is enough to make a skirt are examples of logical abilities.

- ★ *Artistic* (creativity, using artistic talents, using musical talents, using dramatic talents). Being able to draw, write poetry, arrange flowers, play a musical instrument, take photographs, sing, or design an outfit are all uses of artistic talents.

- ★ *Mechanical* (understanding relationships between parts of machines, making things work). Fixing the motor of an automobile, putting a radio back together, unjamming a sewing machine, and even driving a car all use mechanical strengths.

- ★ *Numerical* (working with numbers). Solving math problems, determining how many miles a car travels per gallon of gasoline, or doubling a recipe to feed eight instead of four are examples of numerical abilities.

- ★ *Clerical* (arranging and recording number and letter combinations). Alphabetizing or putting items in a special order, filling, and typing are all clerical skills.

- ★ *Spatial* (understanding how parts of things fit together, multidimensional). Being able to put together a jigsaw puzzle, rearranging furniture attractively in a room, and putting together a model airplane all use spatial understanding.

- ★ *Physical* (bodily strength and coordination, manual dexterity). Lifting weights, enjoying aerobic exercise, pushing furniture, and hanging up pictures in a straight line all use physical skills.

- ★ *Organizational* (planning, implementing, evaluating). Planning a party or conducting a meeting makes use of organizational abilities.

Continued on Next Page

★ ***Intellectual*** (original thinking, seeking knowledge, thinking ahead). Reading a mystery novel and deciding "the butler did it," studying for an exam, and analyzing the problem in making a car repair are examples of using intellectual skills.

Entrepreneurs use their aptitudes to help them develop their business ideas into business realities. They may use mechanical aptitudes to open a radio repair shop, organizational talents to decide which customer's radio to fix first, and artistic aptitudes to design a sign for their business. However, entrepreneurs usually select a business area in which they have an interest. This you will read about in the next section.

Personal Profile 4

Experience and Aptitudes

On the left-hand portion of the following chart, briefly describe two important experiences you have had. On the other side, list the aptitudes you used in the experience, or those you gained from the experience, with the terms that best fit from the unit. As you recall, aptitudes refer to a natural talent or inclination for certain activities. Try to remember as many details from your experiences as possible. You may be surprised at some of the aptitudes you used.

EXPERIENCE	APTITUDES
Example: I found my grandparent's old oak kitchen set in the attic. I stripped off the old paint on the table until I reached the natural wood. After refinishing it, I had a beautiful new kitchen set to give to my brother and his new wife for a wedding present.	1. Spatial 2. Artistic 3. Physical
1.	1. 2. 3.
2.	1. 2. 3.

What Experiences Have I Had?

Personal Profile 5

Aptitudes Worksheet

Review the list of aptitudes that appear in this unit. Select at least three that you feel you have. List at least two reasons/activities you do that support your claim. Try to be detailed in providing an explanation for why you feel you have a certain aptitude.

APTITUDES	REASONS
Example: Artistic	1. I like to draw pictures of people I know.
	2. I enjoy playing the piano whenever I can.
1.	1.
	2.
2.	1.
	2.
3.	1.
	2.

What Are Your Interests?

An interest is a subject that you like to read about, hear about, or find exciting. Often, a person will develop an interest into a hobby. He or she will spend his or her spare time doing an activity that is enjoyable and relaxing. Generally, interests fit a person's personality, knowledge/skills, life-style, and values. You may be very interested in some things or have little or no interest in other things.

Interests can be general but included within broad categories such as cooking, farming, construction, athletics, reading, or cars. Or, interests can be specific, with examples such as the following: dessert making, dairy farming, furniture refinishing, jogging, reading spy thrillers, or collecting old car parts.

Interests or hobbies often develop because of a person's aptitude for such activities. An individual with a strong artistic aptitude may greatly enjoy cake

Continued on Next Page

decorating. Because of a natural talent, this person may become interested in knowing as much as possible about the activity. He or she may make a lot of cakes for many occasions while developing the interest into a hobby.

Often, a hobby can become a full-fledged business. Paul Newman is a famous actor known for his blue eyes, but he also enjoys cooking, Now, he is well-known for his salad dressing, which can be found on many grocery store shelves. In addition, actress Jane Fonda, well known for many of her movie roles, is an avid exerciser. Many recognize her face on workout clothing, records, videos, and books. She turned her exercise and aerobics hobby into a well-paying business. Certainly, the number of ideas future entrepreneurs can develop is limited only by the limits of their imagination.

Personal Profile 6

Experience-Interests

Carefully review each experience listed and described in Profile 4. What interests are captured in each? List these below. An interest is a feeling that goes along with special attention to a subject important to you. You may discover after completing this worksheet that you have many more interests than you thought. If any of your interests have developed into hobbies, be sure to include these on your list.

1.

2.

3.

Personal Profile 7

Interests Grouped According to Similarities

Look at the interests you listed in Profile 6 and place them into groups according to similarities. List the groupings below.

What Knowledge Is Important to an Entrepreneur?

An individual who considers entrepreneurship needs to develop several areas of business knowledge. Knowledge is a familiarity or understanding of a subject gained through experience or through learning and study. You might gain knowledge in the following ways:

★ Learn about the **community**. What kinds of people live in it, what age groups, whether there are married or single people, what is the number of families, and what are the income levels.

★ Know **what is happening.** What are the latest styles in fashion, what foods do people eat, what new services are in demand, what types of exercise are now popular. Basically, an entrepreneur will want to know whatever is new and different.

★ Gain knowledge through **education**. Each subject you study in school will be important as an entrepreneur, including mathematics, history, languages bookkeeping, auto mechanics, home economics, marketing, agriculture production, and English literature.

★ Learn **on the job**. That job in your vocational area is providing you with practical experience and knowledge every day.

Definitely, all of the knowledge that an individual acquires throughout her or his lifetime is important to becoming an entrepreneur. **Entrepreneurship combines all an individual's knowledge and experience.**

Interests

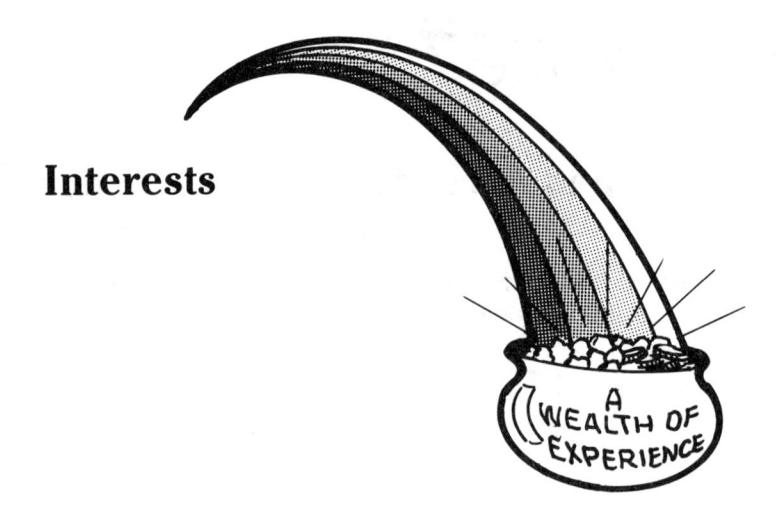

Someone with retail work experience, a love of history, and interest in old things may find that an antique store would be popular in a community. Such a business combines experience, interests, and hobbies.

A person who loves cross-country skiing could find that he or she might become an entrepreneur by teaching this skill to others, by organizing and planning trips for those who want to learn this hobby, or by purchasing and renting equipment. Certainly, if you have an interest, you may find that much of the knowledge you have developed enhances that interest.

What Skills Will I Need as an Entrepreneur?

Entrepreneurs need many skills to successfully run a business. Being able to apply successfully the knowledge acquired and demonstrate it in running a business shows the *skill* level acquired by the entrepreneur. These skills differ somewhat from business to business, because each business is different. Certainly, each business will have some special knowledge and skills needed for it alone. However, there are also general skills and knowledge common to most businesses. Some general areas follow:

* *Developing a business plan.* This is a proposal that describes your business and serves as a guide to manage your business. Most often, the business plan is important if you need to borrow money or want people to invest in your business.

* *Obtaining technical assistance.* Getting help from experienced people and specialized agencies can given entrepreneurs added knowledge and skill to make decisions.

* *Choosing the type of ownership.* How a business is organized legally depends on how it is owned. If one person owns it, it is a *sole proprietorship*. If more than one share in owning-managing the business, it is a *partnership*. A *corporation* is chartered by the state and operates as a legal entity separate from its owners.

* *Planning the market strategy.* This is a business tool to help plan and coordinate all of the activities involved in the exchange of goods and services between producers and consumers.

- ★ **Locating the business.** This is a very important decision that can "make" or "break" a new business. The small business owner must select the "right" site for the business.

- ★ **Financing the business.** It may be necessary to know where to go to borrow the money needed to start your business and keep it going.

- ★ **Dealing with legal issues.** The entrepreneur deals with a variety of legal questions. He or she needs to know when to seek advice and where to get this advice.

- ★ **Complying with government regulations.** Government laws exist to protect everyone involved in business—the citizens who work for the business, consumers, business owners, and even the environment. Regulations concerning small business operation are made on the federal, state, county, and local levels.

- ★ **Managing the business.** Good management is the key to success. Managers must plan the work of the business, organize people and resources for work, staff the business, direct employees, and control and evaluate work.

- ★ **Managing human resources.** This involves working with people so they will be good employees. Human resource management involves planning, organizing, directing, and evaluating all the activities that directly involve employees and promote their productivity.

- ★ **Promoting the business.** Informing consumers about the products and services of a business to help them make a good purchase decision is the purpose of promotion.

- ★ **Managing sales efforts.** It is very important to use good selling principles to attract new customers as well as to continue to serve old customers. If a firm cannot sell its products or services, it will not make a profit and the business will fail.

- ★ **Keeping the business records.** Keeping business records is a form of score keeping. Small business owners/managers can know the current score of their business with accurate and up-to-date records.

- ★ **Managing the finances.** This is needed for a business to grow and earn profits. Financial management tasks include reading and analyzing financial statements and then using this information to determine the strengths and weaknesses of the firm. Financial statements give information needed to plan and take necessary corrective action.

- ★ **Managing customer credit and collection.** Owners of small businesses often must extend credit to customers so that sales will not be lost. At the same time, they must avoid ending up with long overdue accounts that can tie up capital and increase collection costs. Customer credit is given to those people whose financial backgrounds have been checked for payment of obligations. Collections refers to the method or schedule used for payment.

- ★ **Protecting the business.** It is necessary to identify the risks faced by entrepreneurs by business crime or property loss. In addition, precautions such as insurance should be taken so that a small firm can lessen its losses due to risks.

What Experiences Have I Had?

Personal Profile 8

Your Experiences Develop Skills

Instructions: Categories are provided on this form to develop a partial inventory of the many skills you already have. Focus on skills that would be helpful in operating your own business. You may have gained these skills at home, on the job, or in school. Beside each skill list where you learned it. You may be surprised to see how important all of your experiences are in acquiring valuable skills.

1. **Handling Money**

   Specific Tasks:　　　　　　　　　How learned:

2. **Getting Along with Others**

   Specific Tasks:　　　　　　　　　How learned:

3. **Selling**

   Specific Tasks:　　　　　　　　　How learned:

4. **Organizing**

   Specific Tasks:　　　　　　　　　How learned:

5. **Directing Activities**

   Specific Tasks:　　　　　　　　　How learned:

How Does an Entrepreneur Gain Expertise?

As you can see, entrepreneurs combine their aptitudes, interests, and the experiences and knowledge they have acquired. They develop skill in a chosen area and demonstrate this skill in running a business. **A high level of skill in an area leads to expertise.**

As an example, when you first learned to ride a bicycle you probably could not balance yourself on two wheels. Pretty soon, with practice and the experiences of falling off, you learned to travel without as much difficulty. However, you still had to learn to watch where you were going, how to steer, how to brake, and how to stop. As you developed knowledge about what you were doing, you began to notice that your skills were improving. Finally, watching what was ahead, steering, and all the other skills you had acquired became nearly automatic. You developed an expertise in managing a bicycle.

Evaluating your experiences, assessing your aptitudes and interests, and developing your knowledge and skills teach you some things about yourself. When you consider the combination of all these things, you may begin to see some entrepreneurial possibilities. It is not necessary to make a career decision yet. You still need to learn more about entrepreneurship.

Are You Building Career Expertise?

Evaluating your experiences provides you with a better sense of the skills and knowledge you possess. In this section, you also learned to assess your aptitudes and identify interests important to you. In addition, you read about different types of skills and knowledge that are important to being a successful entrepreneur.

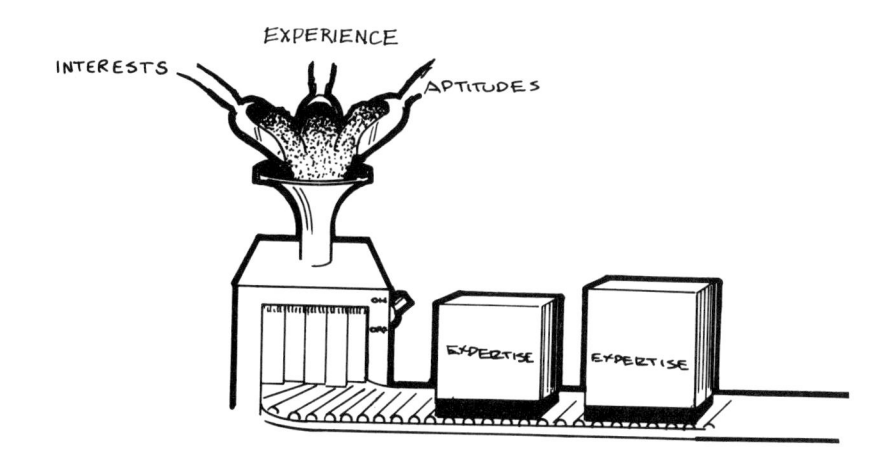

Continued on Next Page

What Experiences Have I Had?

Have you begun to think about entrepreneurial possibilities for yourself? Do you have a career goal that uses your current skills and interests? Or, is it necessary for you to develop greater expertise in a certain area? Certainly you need not make a career decision right away. You still need to learn more about entrepreneurship.

Activities

The following activities are designed to help you learn more about yourself. When you have analyzed your experiences, you may discover how you developed some of your interests. In addition, you will be able to evaluate your aptitudes and see how you apply them every day. Perhaps, you will discover an aptitude that you never before considered! Certainly, you will obtain more information about your entrepreneurial option.

Aptitudes: Matching

Instructions: This worksheet will help you understand that many examples of each aptitude exist. Also, you will see that each aptitude is used in many common everyday situations.

- **a. numerical**
- **b. logical**
- **c. spatial**
- **d. physical**
- **e. clerical**
- **f. organizational**
- **g. mechanical**
- **h. artistic**
- **i. verbal comprehension**
- **j. intellectual**
- **k. verbal or nonverbal communications**

_____ 1. weight lifting

_____ 2. making change for a customer

_____ 3. creating an advertisement

_____ 4. interpreting for a Russian ambassador

_____ 5. reporting the news

_____ 6. predicting the weather

_____ 7. diagnosing a car problem

_____ 8. writing a story

_____ 9. packing a box

_____ 10. planning a class party

What Experiences Have I Had?

_____ 11. typing a letter

_____ 12. moving living room furniture

_____ 13. alphabetizing note cards by the subject's first letter

_____ 14. obtaining directions to Youngstown, Ohio

_____ 15. playing the piano

_____ 16. learning to drive a stick shift car

_____ 17. putting together a jigsaw puzzle

_____ 18. making a funny face

_____ 19. making a class schedule for second semester

_____ 20. fixing a lawn mower

_____ 21. studying for an exam

_____ 22. putting together a cake shaped like a clown

_____ 23. sorting buttons by shape and color

_____ 24. figuring out the end of a story before reading the last chapter

_____ 25. yelling at a football game

_____ 26. rolling your eyes

_____ 27. performing a song/dance routine

_____ 28. thinking about what you should answer to an exam question

_____ 29. working for an auto repair shop

_____ 30. coming to a conclusion after being given certain facts

_____ 31. solving a math problem

_____ 32. planning a schoolwide event

_____ 33. reacting to a telephone request

_____ 34. complaining because you are cold

_____ 35. making out a calendar with your activities for the next week

What Experiences Have I Had?

Aptitude Exploration

Instructions: After reviewing the following aptitudes and examples, choose four aptitudes that best describe your strengths and write two personal examples of experiences upon which you based your answer

Aptitudes   Personal Examples

Verbal or nonverbal communication
- Talking on the phone for long periods.
- Nodding your head or shrugging your shoulders, talking without words.

Verbal comprehension
- Following instructions on an exam.
- Dressing for rain after hearing the weather report.

Logical
- Figuring out how to get into the house when you do not have the key.
- Solving a mystery before finishing the book, because of the clues the author left.

Artistic
- Acting in a skit.
- Drawing a sketch.

Mechanical
- Fixing a broken toaster.
- Knowing how to jump-start a car when the battery dies.

Aptitudes   Personal Examples

Numerical
- Measuring ingredients for a cake.
- Calculating how much paint you need to paint a house.

Clerical
- Answering a telephone switchboard and taking messages.
- Using a word processor to write letters.

Spatial
- Designing a birdhouse to fit between two branches of a tree.
- Packing a picnic basket.

Physical
- Participating in sports.
- Kneading bread.

Organizational
- Deciding how you will get all your homework done and go out on Saturday night.
- Directing a meeting.

Intellectual
- Learning your Spanish vocabulary words for a quiz.
- Reading a book of your choice.

Crossword Puzzle

Instructions: This activity will help you review some of the terms you learned in this section. Read the clues and fill in the puzzle.

Across

4. _____ happen when knowledge, skill, or practice occurs through watching or being involved in an event.
7. Aptitude: working with numbers.
8. Successful application of knowledge acquired and demonstration of this knowledge in running a business.
10. Legal organization of a business depends on the type of _____.
13. Aptitude: applying reason to problems.
14. A feeling that goes along with special attention to a subject important to you.
15. Activities that you enjoy doing in your spare time.
16. Aptitude: bodily strength or manual dexterity.
17. Aptitude: spoken words or actions that can tell ideas, emotions, or events.
19. High levels of skill in a certain area.

Down

1. Aptitude: understanding relationships between parts of machines.
2. Aptitude: understanding how parts of things fit together; multidimensional.
3. Understanding or awareness of a subject through learning about it or through an actual experience.
5. Aptitude: arranging and recording number and letter combinations.
6. Employees of a business. (2 words)
9. Aptitude: using creative talents.
10. Aptitude: planning, implementing, evaluating.
11. The method used for paying, or scheduling credit payments.
12. The market _____ is a business tool to help plan and coordinate the activities used in the exchange of goods and services between producers and consumers.
18. Natural talents or inclinations for certain activities.

What Experiences Have I Had?

Interest Search

Instructions: List 10 hobbies that you have enjoyed doing in your life thus far. List at least one reason why you enjoyed each one. Look for common interests that may lead you to become an entrepreneur.

	Hobbies	**Why Enjoyed**
Example:	baking cakes	fun to create something
1.		
2.		
3.		
4.		
5.		
6.		
7.		
8.		
9.		
10.		

What Experiences Have I Had?

Basic Skills for Business Owners

Instructions: All the knowledge that you have gained to the present day will help you in operating a business of your own. Try the following exercises to test one small part of this knowledge. Then discuss with the class the importance of math, reading, and communication skills to business owners.

1. **Problem:** You have decided to sell chocolate chip cookies. You would like to sell 10 dozen cookies per day. Your cost is $1.25 per dozen and you want to make $1.25 per dozen above cost. How much in total dollars will you need to take in per day?

2. Correct any spelling errors that you detect in this memo to a banker.

Memo

To: Mr. Banker
From: I.M. Sucess
 	
   Do to the decrease in interest rates, I would like to refinace our currant 90-day loan at the lowest rate you now have avalable.
 	
   Thank you for your immediate attention to this matter.

3. Number these accounts payable in alphabetical order to simplify your bookkeeping system.

_____ Miller, L.J.   _____ Williams, M.B.

_____ Cook, D.K.   _____ Bayer, E.J.

_____ Johnson, S.A.   _____ Swingle, A.A.

_____ Rollins, D.M.   _____ Kelly, I.L.

_____ LeFever, C.S.   _____ Baughman, O.L.

_____ Yeager, C.S.   _____ Hardesty, R.M.

_____ Bateman, J.S.   _____ Charles, P.E.

Your teacher has a copy of the correct answers to check your work.

Telephone Survey

Call three entrepreneurs who operate businesses related to your vocational area. Ask each of them to name the 10 most important skills needed to operate a business successfully. Compare the answers of all three and list the skills named by all of them. Discuss results in class.

What Experiences Have I Had?

Success Stories

Think about how these entrepreneurs selected their career goals. Answer the questions included with the success stories and then begin section 3.

Name: Dan Rhoades

Business Name: Auto Body Specialty's

Business Address: 8020 N. Dixie Drive
Dayton, OH 45414

Business Phone: (513) 898-7272

Type of Business: Auto body repair and painting

When Dan Rhoades was 20 years old, he started Auto Body Specialty's. His thorough training at Patterson Co-op High School in Dayton, his rewarding experiences with VICA (Dan won the national VICA auto body contest), and his on-the-job training gave Dan the confidence that he could deal with customers and manage his own shop.

The biggest change Dan sees in his life-style is that he no longer has two or three bosses to answer to or someone breathing down his neck. However, Dan thinks that he's harder on himself than any boss ever was. "Now I have only one boss—myself—and I think this boss is the hardest one to work for." Dan characterizes his life-style by saying it consists of "long hours and hard work."

Dan financed his business through a combination of personal savings plus loans. Because he feels strongly about being his own boss, Auto Body Specialty's is organized as a sole proprietorship. Dan was able to use his experiences as a student at Patterson Co-op High School to determine who his potential customers would be. Locating the business on North Dixie seemed obvious to Danny because of the extra high volume of traffic.

In setting up his business, Dan received assistance from a variety of contacts and resources. Friends who work at parts and paint supply stores, people he met while working at other auto body shops, and the faculty and principal at Patterson Co-op High School were all of help. Still, there were problems: how to get the necessary equipment, building, customers, and employees. Being able to borrow money and advertising solved the first three problems. Finding good employees, according to Dan, ". . . is always an ongoing problem."

Currently, Dan needs a larger building and needs to increase the number of employees so he can give more time to managing the business. Normally, Dan employs two other people, but right now he has just one employee, a young man who also graduated from Patterson Co-op High School.

Continued on Next Page

At this time, all of the profits go back into the business. Sales were lower than projected last year because of a two month slow period, which all the auto body shops in the area experienced.

Dan feels that the technical as well as academic skills he gained as a student at Patterson Co-op have contributed to his success, even though academics were hard initially. His strong marketing ability, his abilities to get along with people, be flexible, and put in long hours, and his resourcefulness all contribute to his success as an entrepreneur.

To Dan, "it has always been very satisfying to assemble a wrecked car back to its original shape." Dan also derives great satisfaction from doing a quality job and satisfying the body repair market. Dan feels that, through hard work, intense planning, and maximizing his potential, he can reach his goals.

Dan said that, one day, he would like to be able to retire, buy a yacht, and take plenty of vacations. As to when he will consider himself a success, Dan will say only that ". . . success will catch me off guard one day."

In addition to his education at Patterson Co-op, Dan attended Dupont Refinishing School, which was the prize for winning the national VICA auto body contest. He currently is attending a car unibody workshop.

Case Study Questions

Dan Rhoades
Auto Body Specialty's

1. What experiences gave Dan the confidence to become an entrepreneur?

2. Which aptitudes listed in this section apply to Dan?

3. What type of business ownership did Dan select, and why?

4. What does Dan say about finding good employees?

5. Do you think that Dan tries to improve his skills? Why or why not?

....

Name: John R. Miller

Business Name: Bryant Hill Jerseys

Business Address: 100 Bryant Street
Chesterfield, MA 01012

Business Phone: (413) 296-4400

Type of Business: Dairy farm

John Miller's roots go back 200 years in the town of Chesterfield, Massachusetts. He chose to start his own dairy and Jersey cattle breeding business partly as a way to maintain that heritage.

John's grandfather was a dairy farmer. His mother's family had farmed in Chesterfield for generations, though the family farm was sold before John decided to go into business.

John had operated his own egg business from the age of 10. From age 12, he was involved in 4-H projects breeding registered Jersey cattle. At school he maintained a "respectable" grade level, he says. He was active in 4-H and FFA (Future Farmers of America) activities and held both local and state offices. He is still an assistant 4-H leader.

These activities gave John experience in public speaking and debate that has proven valuable in business. He belongs also to nonagricultural civic groups in Chesterfield. He believes it's good public relations.

John majored in animal science at Smith Vocational High School in Northampton, Massachusetts. He also attended the State University of New York at Delhi, New York, for one semester and took artificial insemination instruction at the University of Massachusetts, Amherst, Massachusetts.

This formal training "taught me many techniques in dairy herd management, record keeping, ration balancing, soil management, crop growing, financial projecting, and other aspects of farm management so extremely essential in successfully getting a dairy business off the ground," John says.

Continued on Next Page

In addition to producing high-quality milk, John's Jersey herd has been a consistent winner in breed competition, and he sells breeding stock in all parts of the country. John likes being his own boss because he can make decisions to improve the breed. He has two local dairy farms as competition. However, the other two do not sell breeding stock. John believes his stock sales give him a shield against the ups and downs of the milk market.

When he first went in business, many dairy farmers favored Holsteins. But John had faith in his Jerseys, and he finds the popularity pendulum is now swinging in his direction. "I've shown my lenders that Jersey cows are efficient dairy cows worthy of investment," he says. "The farm's roughage program has more than doubled through land improvements. I set production and classification goals for the herd, and we've surpassed them."

Though John is now a sole proprietor, that is not the form of business he originally preferred. He tried to go into partnership with a couple of other dairymen "in hopes that I wouldn't have to have such a great cash outlay," he says. The partnership didn't work out. John had to finance his farm with a large mortgage. "It wasn't what I really wanted to do at first, but it's worked out okay," he says.

Last year's sales amounted to about $135,000, and half John's profits were put back into the business. With milk prices down, this has been a break-even year so far. John hopes for "a year good enough so I can make a solid profit," because he'd like to be more secure financially and there are several land and building improvements he'd like to carry out.

John is finding out firsthand that farming carries more risk than other businesses. He says he tries to learn from his mistakes but recognizes that "lots of times there are things that are just not my fault as far as uncertainties in the marketplace and prices and things of that nature."

One thing entrepreneurship demands is that he "be more flexible with finances and be willing to put more back into the business than into the household."

John's advice to anyone contemplating starting his own business is to know what he's getting into. "If you can get involved working with someone or for someone before you decide to take the big plunge—unless you already have a lot of experience from your background or upbringing—I think that's a very good place for starters."

Case Study Questions

John R. Miller
Bryant Hill Jerseys

1. How did John Miller's family background figure in his decision to become a dairy farmer?

What Experiences Have I Had?

2. What were his early entrepreneurship and agricultural experiences?

3. How did vocational, college, and technical training help him reach his career goal?

4. How does his stock breeding and sales program help reduce the ups and downs of dairy farming?

5. Why would John have preferred a partnership to start with?

....

Name: Anna T. McLaughlin

Business Name: Professional Plant Care Service

Business Address: 1346 Old River Road
Manville, RI 02838

Business Phone: (401) 765-3606 or (401) 333-8748
Type of Business: Interior landscaping

Anna McLaughlin says, "There would be no business without my vocational education. It gave me the knowledge of horticulture and showed me how to work with my hands—to get dirty."

While in high school at Davies Vocational Technical School, Lincoln, Rhode Island, Anna majored in horticulture. Her training included plant identification, plant requirements, ornamental horticulture, plant and soil sciences, pest control, and greenhouse management. She developed self-confidence and assertiveness as her knowledge grew, and through her involvement with Future Farmers of America (FFA) she learned leadership.

Continued on Next Page

Anna combined her horticultural skills with an artistic nature in selecting the type of business to open. Says Anna, "I saw many people in offices, banks, and restaurants creating their own indoor gardens, often losing their costly purchases." She noted a need for professional care of indoor plants while working for a wholesale florist, where customers often asked her questions about plant selection and care.

At age 24, Anna started her own business. She states, "I couldn't find the kind of job I wanted. I knew interior landscaping was challenging, and I believed I could do the job." She targeted her potential customers as new businesses, existing businesses with neglected plants, and new public buildings, many of which "are built with the addition of indoor plants in mind." Anna began her business at night while working for someone else. She used money from her job to purchase the van needed for transporting plants.

It wasn't easy for Anna to establish a reputation in the field, but she persevered. She says, "I believe in doing the best I can and having a positive attitude. I have faith in myself."

Professional Plant Care Service is a full-service interior landscaping firm. Anna designs interior landscapes and selects the plants based on light, temperature, water requirements, durability and visual effect. She then services the plants weekly, guaranteeing their health and appearance.

Anna feels that being a small business gives her an edge on competition. "I can oversee all major work and devote more time and care to each job." Professional Plant Care Service is a sole proprietorship employing five people. Anna proudly states that all of her employees are students from her high school. She trains them for a career and hopes they, in turn, will do the same for someone else one day.

In the future, Anna hopes to double her business while maintaining the personal service she provides. She says, "I want to hire enough people to oversee jobs that the business can run itself."

Anna enjoys the independence and sense of accomplishment that come with owning her own company. "I love it when someone says, 'That's beautiful!' and keeping it that way is my job—a challenge."

Case Study Questions

Anna T. McLaughlin
Professional Plant Care Service

1. Where did Anna McLaughlin get the idea for her business? How did she target potential customers?

Continued on Next Page

2. What are the necessary skills in her business, and how did she acquire them?

3. Owning one's own business involves total responsibility. Anna's responsibility does not end with choosing and planting the plants. What else does it entail and how does she fulfill it?

4. To Anna, what are the advantages of being a small business?

5. What are Anna's business goals?

The Think Tank

What Experiences Have I Had?

Instructions: Summarize what you have learned in this section by answering the following questions as a private journal entry to keep for use in your future career planning. Add it to the same activity from section 1.

☞ What is experience?

☞ What types of aptitudes might you have?

☞ What are your interests?

☞ What knowledge is important to an entrepreneur?

☞ What skills will you need as an entreprenuer?

☞ How does an entrepreneur gain expertise?

☞ Can you choose a career goal?

Section 3
What Type of Business Could I Start?

Completing this section will help you—

* identify types of businesses related to your area of vocational training

* identify a business you might start based on your interests, skills, and hobbies

* identify a potential business idea

* assess the business needs of the community

"Perhaps imagination is only intelligence having fun."

—George Scialabba
in Harvard Magazine

What Is This Section About?

Up to now, you have looked at your personal potential to start a business. However, a successful business is not built on personal characteristics alone. In this section we will consider the business ideas and concept of innovations and creativity.

What Is a Business Idea?

A business idea is the combination of a person's experience, skills, market (customers), and product or service.

A business idea can be original (McDonald's was the first fast-food restaurant), an improvement on someone else's idea (Wendy's), or the transplant of an idea from another community to your own (Famous Amos Cookies in California, Cheryl's Cookies in Ohio).

Can you name five unique or creative businesses in your community? Describe how each is unique.

Where Do You Get Your Business Idea?

What comes to mind when you think about an idea? Is it a light bulb overhead? **Ideas can come from thinking there must be a better way.** Business ideas also may develop from the following:

* ***Service needed by others.*** You may have developed skills or have an interest in an activity that someone would gladly pay you to do for them. For example, many people feel it necessary to see a hairstylist. A student who loves dogs could take care of the pets of families that go on vacation.

* ***Entertainment.*** Providing entertainment as a clown at children's birthday parties could become a business. Someone who enjoys singing might put together an act for a popular restaurant. Or what about offering an entertaining cooking class that people attend to have fun and learn?

* ***Marketing the products of others.*** Students who always enjoyed selling magazines or Girl Scout cookies might consider a business in which they promote and sell someone else's products or services. An individual could market Black & Decker tools or gourmet cooking equipment as an entrepreneurial enterprise.

* ***Repair services.*** Many people need the services of an electrician or auto repair person after all the shops and offices are closed. An enterprising person may choose to start a business that operates during off-hours. An entrepreneur might develop a pickup and delivery service for customers who need something repaired, but have difficulty getting to a repair shop except during "regular" business hours.

* ***New inventions.*** A student tired of using a certain shop tool because it is slow may invent a new tool that is more effective and quicker to use. A business could develop from that idea. An entrepreneur may take everyday articles such as scissors, knives, and even a wrench and convert them for use by left-handed people. Marketing products to this population could become a business.

* ***Extension of hobbies.*** A home economics student who has a hobby of buying silk scraps and making men's and women's ties and scarves may find there is a huge demand for such products. A food-services student who always seems to be a short-order cook at home may decide to develop a business out of this hobby.

* ***Interests.*** An agriculture student who has an interest in plants and reads all he or she can about plant diseases may start a business as a plant doctor. In addition, an aerobics exercise enthusiast may choose to start aerobics exercise classes for other people interested in getting in shape.

* ***Product improvement.*** An agriculture student who loves birds may discover that the usual manufactured birdseed does not attract as large a variety of birds as does the feed he or she mixes. Perhaps a gourmet feed business will be born. Who knows?

* ***New technologies.*** A business education student who develops skill in computer uses may decide to open a word-processing service or develop computer software with a computer at home.

You probably have ideas for businesses that you never really thought about. Many of us are nervous with creative thinking because past recognition—school grades, parental approval, job reviews, and so forth—depended on having the right answer. **Learning how to be creative and generate ideas takes practice.**

For the purpose of creative thinking, select an object in the room such as a pencil, desk, milk carton, computer disk, thumbtack, wastebasket, or jacket. Write down as *many* different uses for that object as you can think of in 10 minutes. Do not judge your ideas, just write them down.

How many ideas did you come up with? Try it with another object and see if you can come up with more ideas than you did the first time.

What Business Ideas Can You Think of Related to Using Your Vocational Training?

Many entrepreneurs start businesses using their experiences. Thus, ideas often pop into people's heads from seeing things done poorly or from creating a new use for skills they are using on their present job.

Vocational education gives you a head start—both in moving into a job of your choice and in moving closer to finding an idea for starting your own business.

- Creative new businesses have been started by auto mechanics students who opened businesses outside of school. They found a market for those big, old cars that had quality, but needed repair to bring a high sales profit.

- Consider the cosmetology student who created a business by visiting nursing homes and providing beauty care for the aged. There was quite a need, no investment was required for a shop, and there were profits to be made.

- An ordinary business was made unique by an agricultural education graduate who also used the dairy farm as a "farm zoo" for families with small children.

- Several business and office students have paid their way through college by typing papers and reports. The need is there once you establish a customer list.

- What about the marketing education student who prepares newspaper advertisements for local merchants? The student lives in a small town that has no advertising agencies.

- Successful businesses have been started by home economics students who move their "restaurant" to a large plant or office building at lunchtime. Time and parking don't allow employees to go out for lunch, so the students bring lunch to the work site.

Most vocational programs lend themselves to creative business start-ups.
Sometimes we overlook the opportunity to be a job maker—not just a job taker.

Personal Profile 9

Businesses Based on Your Vocational Experience

Take time to consider some creative businesses in your vocational area. Think of all the possible businesses for which you might start using your vocational experiences as a base. Don't worry about whether you have the financing for this. This is your chance to dream on paper. List as many ideas as you can. Don't worry about how ridiculous they may seem. Just let your imagination work freely.

After you have your list, find a partner to talk with about your creative ideas. See how many different ideas you can come up with together. The entire class may wish, then, to see which pair had the most ideas (not necessarily the best).

How Can Interests, Skills, and Hobbies Lead to a Business Idea?

(Thought bubble: LANDSCAPING, REPAIR SHOP, BAKERY, TYPING POOL, DELIVERY SERVICE, HOBBY SHOP, SILK FLOWERS, BALLOON SHOP)

Entrepreneurs are enthusiastic, positive people who love what they are doing. In fact, most of them say that the thrill of making their idea successful is more important than how much money they make. Many are willing to work for next to nothing just to be able to be the boss in a business they really enjoy.

So, the things you have liked doing all your life are natural opportunities for business creation. Imagine yourself spending 10 hours a day in your favorite activity—and making money, too!

For example:

- Collecting butterflies and turning them into decorative items
- Hiking through the woods offering guided tours
- Refinishing furniture
- Farming and selling produce
- Arranging flowers
- Repairing small engines such as lawn mowers
- Making and selling crochet or needlepoint items
- Baking cakes and pastries
- Planning parties
- Creating the makeup looks for individuals on special occasions
- Framing and selling your photographs for profit that you take and develop for fun

What Type of Business Could I Start?

Personal Profile 10

Businesses Based on Your Interests, Skills, and Hobbies

Take a few minutes to recall the interests, skills, and hobbies that you identified in section 2. Think about all the possible businesses you might start using your interests, skills, and hobbies. List as many creative ideas for business ventures as possible.

Compare the two lists of business ideas you developed in Profile activity 9 and this profile. Are there any businesses on either list that combine both your interests/skills/hobbies and your educational experience? Circle them on your lists.

What Business Might You Start Someday?

Most of today's entrepreneurs had no opportunity to think about starting a business when they were in high school. They probably wouldn't have believed it possible to be where they are today if someone had asked them to think about it.

This is your chance to think big! There is no reason for you to limit your career options right now. Let's pretend that you will be able to start your own business sometime in the future.

Personal Profile 11

My Business

Envision yourself as a successful entrepreneur while completing this activity. Pick your favorite business from the items you just circled. Answer the following questions based on your favorite item.

1. What is the name of your business?

2. What kind of business is it?

3. What makes your business the best?

4. Where is your business located—at home, downtown, in a suburban mall?

Continued on Next Page

5. What kind of customers are attracted to your business? Do you sell a product or service to homemakers, working women and men, children, music lovers, mechanics and so forth?

6. How is your business related to your vocational area of study?

7. Do you use any of your aptitudes or interests in your business? Which ones?

8. What are your total yearly gross sales?

9. How many employees work for you?

10. What hours is your business open?

Why Should You Know about Your Community?

Every business succeeds or fails depending on the needs of the surrounding area. The type of business depends on the size of the area . . . but whether it is a manufacturer, a retailer, or a service business, pleasing *enough* customers is what business is all about. How do you think a woolens store would do in southern Florida, for example?

It's not enough to have a great idea for a business. You must have a reason to believe that people need your product and will want it instead of the competition's items. Smart business planners know all about their community.

Let's be business planners by thinking about the important characteristics (or demographics) of your area. Define your *market area* by determining how far you would travel as a customer to benefit from the business you are considering.

How Large Is Your Community?

Each business planner must decide what the market area for his or her product or service will be. The market area refers to the distance a customer would travel to buy from you. The market area varies with the type of product or service you offer. How far would you go to buy a loaf of bread? A pair of shoes? A new car?

Procter and Gamble, manufacturer of products such as Crisco and Jif peanut butter, often considers customers across the entire country. In some cases, this company considers its market area as being the world. Wendy's began business in Columbus, Ohio, but as it grew, its owners had to learn about many other communities. Wendy's market area has grown very large.

Why Should You Know about the People?

Business planners always consider important population characteristics, or demographics, of a market area. Information about the people who live in your market area can be obtained from marketing surveys. Such surveys present all sorts of information gathered on people, usually in statistical form, such as age, sex, income, family size, etc.

Continued on Next Page

Information can be gathered in various ways—from written questionnaires, telephone interviews, or computerized data, for example. The U.S. Bureau of the Census is one government agency that collects information on citizens of the United States in its survey every few years. However, a potential entrepreneur may be more interested in a marketing survey such as the one compiled annually by *Sales And Marketing Management* magazine.

Called the *Survey of Buying Power*, this document can be found in the main branch of your library or in a university or college library near you. Call ahead to make sure it is there before going to the library. This reference book gives up-to-date information on such population characteristics as income, age groups, and number of individuals in specific ethnic groups, and regional, state, metropolitan area, county, city, and suburban population information.

Why Should You Know about Competition?

If your business sells products or services that are similar to those of another company, your business will be competing for customers in the market area. You will be interested in obtaining and keeping a certain market share. **Market share refers to your part, or share, of the people who will demand your products or services and buy from you instead of your competitor.** Imagine the market area as a pie. Your market share could be three large pieces worth of the entire pie.

You will want to know about your competition to successfully keep your market share. The following questions are a guide in starting to learn more about your competition.

- What sort of products or services does your competition sell? Are they exactly like what you sell, or different? How are they priced? How is the quality of their products or services?

- What types of customers does your competition attract? Are they the same people who come to you? Are they older or younger than your potential customers?

- Where are these businesses located? Are they in the downtown area or in a suburban mall? Are they close to a fast-food strip, or are they in a warehouse district? Is your competition located geographically close to your proposed site? Which site promises to be more convenient to the customers you wish to serve?

- Which businesses seem to be doing well? Can you tell why? How long have they been around? What is their business record?

Knowing your competition will help you make decisions regarding your business. If there are seven bakeries in your area that all make desserts, you may decide that you will sell some desserts, but that you will bake all different flavors of bread. A creative businessperson can develop many ideas to compete successfully with similar businesses. For instance, he or she can change the price charged, offer additional services, or have an easier location to reach. Knowing your competition will help you know your business and how to make it popular with the customers.

Why Should You Know about Changes in Your Community?

Finally, successful entrepreneurs anticipate and react to change. In fact, the real advantage of small business is that it can change more easily to meet the opportunities for success than can a large business.

Some kinds of change that a business planner who thinks ahead needs to know about include the following:

- How is the **population changing** in the area? Is it growing older? Are young people moving away? Are people getting married or being divorced?

- What kind of **business is coming into the area?** How many new jobs will be provided? Are employees skilled or unskilled? Will they be from the area or will they move in from different areas of the country?

- What kinds of **businesses are leaving the area or failing?** Is unemployment increasing? Is it already a problem?

- What businesses are needed because **more women are working?** What can you do for them that they will no longer have time for?

- What do people in the area like to do with **their leisure time?** What types of recreational areas do you have in the area? What hobbies seem to be popular in the area?

- What **new technologies** are being used? Are personal computers being used? Are the hospitals using new medical equipment?

- How does **transportation** help or hinder local business? How are the highways? Are there city buses with easy access to destinations? Is the area spread far apart and connected by highways?

- What is happening to **change whole neighborhoods or major sections of the community?** Do people shop downtown? Are there popular suburban malls? Is there a fast-food strip? Is new industry coming in? Is government housing going up?

Personal Profile 12

Market Area Changes

Focus on the market area for your future business. Evaluate each change in your market area. Indicate whether you see each change as positive (+) or negative (−) for your business. Explain your reasoning.

Continued on Next Page

What Type of Business Could I Start?

Change	What Is Happening in My Market Area (or what might happen soon)	Will It Help (+) or Hurt (−) My Business?
Population change		
New business		
Businesses leaving or failing		
More working women		
More leisure time		
New technologies		
Transportation		
Change in neighborhoods or major community sections		

Why Should You Know about Foreign Business?

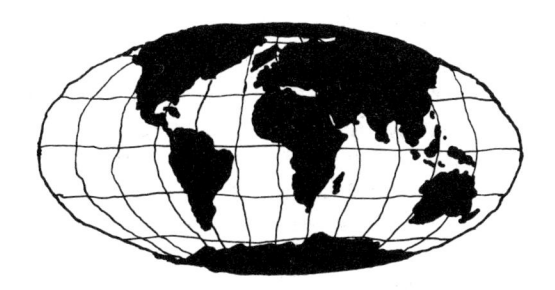

There are over 300 countries on this globe that can provide customers for your products or services. Because you have never been there, it is hard to think about these faraway places as a source of customers for your business idea. For example, China has a population four times the size of the United States. This huge market is just learning about American fashions, Coca-Cola, and apple pie. Doing business with other countries will require that you learn more about their customs, language, and ways of doing business, as well as the process of *exporting*.

Another way to do business with other countries is to buy their products to sell in this country. Such *imports* are growing every year because Americans are impressed with the uniqueness or comparatively low price of foreign products. As the world establishes more and more business connections, there will be unlimited new business opportunities for entrepreneurs.

You may even wish to develop a copy of a foreign product or service to sell in your own area. Sushi, for example, is a Japanese seasoned rice entree often served with raw fish that has become popular in the United States, and now is actually produced in the U.S. Opportunities for such *import substitution* are only as far away as your imagination and your knowledge of countries around the world.

What Sort of Business Might You Start Someday?

In this section, you have thought about what sort of business you might someday like to begin. You learned about the factors an entrepreneur must consider in beginning a business and the changes that can occur in the market area.

You also have read about how a business idea develops. Certainly, it takes practice to be able to come up with new and creative ideas. Vocational education and training definitely help in developing business ideas for potential entrepreneurs. Vocational programs teach students skills and aid in providing actual job experiences. These can later be the springboard to a creative business idea.

The personality of an entrepreneur is usually enthusiastic and positive. These individuals love the work they do and have been able to make their businesses popular and successful.

Before you consider beginning a business, be aware of the demographics of the market area in which you are interested. Awareness of trends and population characteristics will help you plan your business more effectively. Remember, the whole world can be your market.

What Type of Business Could I Start?

Activities

The activities that follow are provided to help you obtain more information on the types of businesses you may wish to start. This section has activities to help you learn how to create a market survey. Someday you might wish to check on the demand for a product or service. Practice in locating the competition on a business map might help you decide where to locate a business. The exercises in understanding changes sometimes faced by businesses and their reaction to such changes should help you in thinking ahead.

Word Scramble

Assessing the Business Needs of the Community

Instructions: Check your understanding of the terms used in this section by completing the following sentences. Unscramble the letters and write the correct words in the spaces.

In addition to having a great idea for a business, you have to have reason to believe that people will MDAEDN[1]_____ your product or service instead of that of the MCPOTTIENOI[2]_____. It is necessary to consider the important characteristics of population, or MRIDOGPECASH[3]

_____.

Certainly, you should have plenty of information about the SCTURMESO[4]

_____ to whom you wish to sell your product or service. You will need to know the number of people in your market area, how many MLFIEAIS[5]

_____ there are, and the number of single adults. It might be important to know a breakdown of age groups. Of course you will want to know

CEIOMN[6]_____ per capita and/or per family. A market survey could include the MISCPAEON[7]_____ that are the primary sources of jobs in the area. You should also know the level of UNECDTAOI[8]

_____ attained: what percentage of the population attended high school or college? Analysis of minority populations in the area should be included in the information on the community as well.

There may be other businesses like the one you are considering. You will need to know about the MNOOCEIPTTI[9]_____: the customers each tries to attract, their location, and whether they are good at what they do. How

CCULSSSEFU[10]_____ are they?

Continued on Next Page

71

What Type of Business Could I Start?

Finally, successful entrepreneurs must be able to anticipate and react to ECANHG[11] _____. You will need to know how the population is changing.

What kinds of businesses are entering or LIGEVAN[12] _____ an area or failing? Are certain businesses now needed because more women are in the work force? What do people in the area like to do with more free or SEUILER[13] _____ time? Are a large number of people out of work or PUENMOLYDE[14] _____? These are just a few of the changes that may be affecting your area.

Entrepreneur Interview Questions

Ask an entrepreneur of your choice the following questions. Based on the responses you receive, write a case study about her or him.

1. Where did you get the idea for your business?

2. Did your interests, skills, and hobbies lead to your business idea?

3. How would you define your market area?

Continued on Next Page

What Type of Business Could I Start?

4. What do you feel is important to know about your customers?

5. What do you know about your competition?

6. What changes have affected your business?

7. What changes do you predict may affect your business in the future?

Estimate

Choose a business in your town or neighborhood. Estimate what the market area is for the business. Phone or visit the manager of the business and ask him or her to define the market area. Write a brief paragraph about what you learned from this activity.

Business Map

List five competing businesses in your area. Draw a map of the business locations or mark their location on a city map. Is there a great demand for this type of business? Does it look like the market areas of the businesses are equally distributed?

Fortune-telling

Describe the changes that will occur in the fast-food industry by the year 2005. How will these changes relate to the society of those times? Determine how you could incorporate those changes into a business.

What Type of Business Could I Start?

Utilizing Opportunities

Instructions: The one thing for sure is that things will always change. Entrepreneurs thrive on change. Peter Drucker suggests that the only way to stay ahead of the rest of the world is to find new and better ways to provide products and services. List at least one possible invention or new business idea for each of the following opportunities.

1. An unusual event, such as the Olympics being held in your hometown.

2. A difference between the way things are and how they ought to be, such as working mothers not having enough time to meet their responsibilities.

3. The need for a different way to do something, such as an easier way to exercise your pet.

4. A change in the market or industry, such as a fad of bicycle racing.

5. Signs of demand changes, such as an increase in foreign foods sales (e.g., McDonald's Chicken McNuggets Shanghai and Mexican fast-food restaurants).

6. Changes in people's attitudes, such as stricter drunk driving laws.

7. New knowledge, such as medical advances that help people live longer.

What Type of Business Could I Start?

Innovation

Instructions: Invent a new product or service. List features (facts) and benefits of your invention below, then give a sales demonstration on it to the class.

Product or Service: _____

Features: **Benefits:**

_____   _____

_____   _____

_____   _____

_____   _____

_____   _____

_____   _____

_____   _____

_____   _____

_____   _____

_____   _____

_____   _____

_____   _____

_____   _____

_____   _____

_____   _____

Field Assignment

Instructions: Go to a local department store and find five products that are being marketed to our country from other countries. Be sure products are from at least three other countries. Give possible reasons customers may choose to buy these products instead of American-made products.

Product: **Reasons:**

1. _____ _____

2. _____ _____

3. _____ _____

4. _____ _____

5. _____ _____

International Markets Exhibit

Instructions: Using the space provided, develop a plan for an exhibit that will illustrate the market needs and cultural issues that Americans selling goods and services in a specific foreign country should consider. Choose one country and focus on the unique differences of that country. Consider the language, dress, rituals, religion, women's roles, and so forth. Implement your plan in a small group. Set up the exhibits in the school cafeteria and invite the entire school to review the exhibition.

What Type of Business Could I Start?

Success Stories

As you read the following case studies, think about how these young successes developed their business ideas and how they were helped by their vocational education. Answer the questions that follow as thoughtfully as possible.

Name: David B. Hansley

Business Name: Hansley Burglar Bars Welding Service

Business Address: 4225 Kataenca Drive South
Jacksonville, FL 32209

Business Phone: (904) 384-0876

Type of Business: Welded security devices

At age 24, David Hansley faces an uphill battle as he starts his welding business.

He has prepared carefully and expensively for this venture, taking basic welding and welding fundamentals at Westside Skill Center, Jacksonville, Florida, and welding technology at Jacksonville Community College. Additionally, he had several months of welding training in the service, at Naval Training Technical Center in California.

He's also held several jobs in production control and warehousing, shipping and receiving of aircraft parts. He's worked on construction jobs for water, sewer, and utility companies, laying and welding pipe. This work experience has taught him familiarity with local building codes.

David's job experience has also taught him that he will be able to go further if he's self-employed. Though he's thankful for the training these jobs have given him, he feels that "you never seem to benefit from all of the effort that you put in. No matter how much you do," he says, "they're only going to let you go so far."

As a young black trained extensively in welding, David felt "if I could do the job for them, there must be some way that I could apply these talents and be able to do the job for myself."

He even feels that being self-employed will give him a kind of security that he couldn't have working for someone else. "People's minds change," he notes. "You can be in a good position and think you've got it made, and the next thing you know, management changes and you're out."

He's aware that in his city, both homeowners and businesses are a growing market for welded security devices such as window bars and storm doors. He also knows that he's competing with older established companies in supplying this demand. "A lot of them have been established for 12, 15, and 20 years," he notes. Just starting out, he won't be able to work as fast or charge as much as these competitors.

Continued on Next Page

Lack of capital is another hurdle. Security welding is an area that he can go into in a small way and build up. He says, "I've got to go into an area that I can afford to go into. I don't have $2,000 to $5,000 in the bank to be buying equipment."

Business zoning codes create a problem. To rent a shop or office in a building zoned for his type of business is too expensive right now. Therefore, David is looking for a piece of land that he can afford to purchase and build his own shop. When that is achieved, he can start advertising his service.

Future possibilities, as the business grows, are to branch into alarm systems and to produce welded items like garden tools for retail. Eventually he'd like to have shops in several different cities.

David thinks he will have to return to school for some business courses and accounting. His warehousing job taught him the importance of good record keeping.

His goal is "basically to live comfortably," he says, "to supply my needs and my family's needs. I'm not trying to be Howard Hughes. I just want to be able to make it and not have to depend on someone else."

David thinks he's making about as much money as he made as an employee. The greatest difference is that he has less free time. When you're employed by someone else, he says, you're not the person "who is forced to sit right here at this desk and type all your reports."

What free time he does have is spent with his wife and their three children. David is a religious person. Much of his spare time revolves around his church. He believes his faith in God has given him "a lot of strength to overcome things that I otherwise would have allowed to be big stumbling blocks."

David is glad he made the choice to work for himself. "It's real shaky sometimes," he says, "but I would rather take the risk now than to wait until later or maybe not even do it and regret that I never tried. I've always learned that it is not so bad to fail, but the bad thing is not to even try."

David's advice to other young entrepreneurs is what was given to him: start small and work up. "You really do have to crawl before you can walk," he says.

Case Study Questions

David B. Hansley
Hansley Burglar Bars Welding Service

1. What was the chief reason David Hansley started his own business?

Continued on Next Page

2. In what way does being self-employed offer greater security than working for someone else?

3. David's advice is, "You have to crawl before you can walk." How is his own business experience demonstrating this?

4. What advantage will owning his own building give him?

5. As a trained welder, David had the skills to start most types of welding business. Why did he choose security bars?

Name: Johanna Michelle Carlson

Business Name: J & R Cafe and Bakery

Business Address: Route 1, Box 222
Superior, WI 54880

Business Phone: (715) 399-8730 or (715) 399-8837

Type of Business: Cafe, bakery, catering

Johanna Carlson started her own business because there were no full-time jobs available in the rural area outside Superior, Wisconsin, where she lived.

Johanna started baking and decorating cakes at the age of 15 to earn money. Her high school program at the Duluth Area Vocational Technical Institute was home

Continued on Next Page

economics. There she learned not only baking skills, but also how to work well with other people.

After high school, Johanna worked for a couple of bakeries before she decided to go out on her own. She saw the need for a bakery in her community. Says Johanna, "People who lived outside Superior had to drive to town for fresh bakery products."

Johanna was independent, had more than her share of common sense, and was determined to succeed. She leveled her savings, cashed in IRAs and CDs, obtained a bank loan, and opened her business at age 22.

She had a lot of help from her family. Proceeds from the sale of their home helped finance the business. Seven members now work for her, including her husband, who also handles the household responsibilities when she can't be at home. In addition, Johanna was helped and supported by the instructor from her vocational school and the president of her bank.

J & R's Cafe seats 50 people, serving hamburgers, sandwiches, and fried foods. The bakery delivers to grocery stores, restaurants, resorts, and gasoline stations. Catering can be handled at the cafe or away. Johanna says, "They can select the food or we will plan the menu ourselves." She feels that what separates her from others in her field is the pride she takes in her business. "It's my business signature," she states.

Running her own business has not been without problems for Johanna. Customers and employees alike felt free to criticize her, and many in the community devalued her business at first "because it was out in the country and they thought it would go nowhere." She has learned to deal with expense control, reduced payroll, menu changes, opening and closing schedules, waste control, overstocking, soaring insurance rates, and especially employees: "family employees, bad employees, lazy employees, employees who want to know what I will do for them, but not what they can do for me."

Johanna is successful because she believes in confronting her problems head-on. When something fails, she takes time to discover why, find the alternative solutions, and try again. Says Johanna, "I take failure, learn from it, put it in its proper perspective, and do it right the next time. I look at failure as one more challenge in life."

J & R Cafe and Bakery is a sole proprietorship. Sales for a recent year were $150,000, and all profits were put back into the business.

Johanna says the everyday experiences in her high school program gave her the know-how, and, "Once I had that, no one could take it away." She describes herself as a hardworking, polite student who was curious about everything. In high school she says she did her own thing. "I didn't try to be a leader, and I know I wasn't a follower. I just wanted to be independent."

Case Study Questions

Johanna Michelle Carlson
J & R Cafe and Bakery

1. What factors helped Johanna determine the type of business she would go into?

2. Johanna's business satisfies several needs and desires. What are they?

3. What aspects of Johanna's character and personality help her in running her own business?

4. What are some of the employee problems Johanna has had to deal with?

5. How does she view failure?

What Type of Business Could I Start?

    Name: DeAlva Gratz Oakes

    Business Name: Alma's

    Business Address: 3771 West Andrew Johnson Highway
                                     Morristown, TN 37814

    Business Phone: (615) 581-8666

    Type of Business: Women's high-fashion clothing store

DeAlva Oakes had a head start on owning her business. Her mother opened it when DeAlva was in school and she helped out in the store from the beginning. Says DeAlva, "My mother has been the key person in my life and my business. She is an extremely hardworking and dedicated woman (who) started the business and worked at getting it all together."

In high school, DeAlva participated in the home economics vocational program at Morristown/Hamblen High School-West in Morristown, Tennessee, where she learned garment construction and was involved with fashion shows.

Following graduation, DeAlva attended the Fashion Institute of America in Atlanta, Georgia, majoring in fashion merchandising, in which she earned an associate's degree. While she felt the lack of training in such subjects as business management, small business accounting, computers, and personnel, DeAlva benefited from her training in public speaking, textiles and fabrics, merchandising, and buying techniques. She states, "I learned the importance of my personal appearance in public, an appreciation of fine-quality fabrics, and the need for budgeting."

With the help of a bank loan, DeAlva became a partner in her mother's business at age 23. Because she could not afford a professional marketing survey, DeAlva simply "assumed the needs were there." In her small community, she offers unique, high-fashion styles previously unavailable to discerning women of all ages. She also stocks accessories such as shoes, handbags, jewelry, and scarves.

DaAlva is aware that in order to succeed she must keep on top of other current trends such as home furnishings, travel, cuisine, and men's clothing. "It all interrelates and has an impact on fashion." She frequently travels to New York City, Dallas, and Atlanta on buying trips in order to survive in the volatile garment industry.

Alma's prides itself in customer courtesy. Says DeAlva, "My employees are trained to make every person who walks in feel recognized, welcome, and very special. I stress 'special' because that's what *we* are."

The business started with two employees and now has eight. Gross sales in a recent year reached $450,000, and 70 percent of profits were reinvested.

As for the future, DeAlva says, "A pipe dream in retail is never to have a markdown." Realistically, however, she hopes to expand the clientele, which will in turn increase sales and profits. DcAlva also wants to open a branch store in . another suitable area.

Continued on Next Page

DeAlva enjoys the rewards of having her own business. She likes the control of selecting her own employees and merchandise, "being surrounded by what I truly love—women's fashion clothing," and knowing there are no limitations on her salary as long as the business continues to expand.

Case Study Questions

DeAlva Gratz Oakes
Alma's

1. Describe the influence of her mother in DeAlva's life.

2. What kinds of formal vocational preparation did DeAlva have for her work?

3. How does she stay up-to-date in an industry that is constantly changing?

4. What makes Alma's special in DeAlva's community?

5. To DeAlva, what are the rewards of being in business for herself?

The Think Tank

What Type of Business Could I Start?

Instructions: Summarize what you have learned in this section by answering the following questions. Keep this as a private journal entry to use in your future career planning.

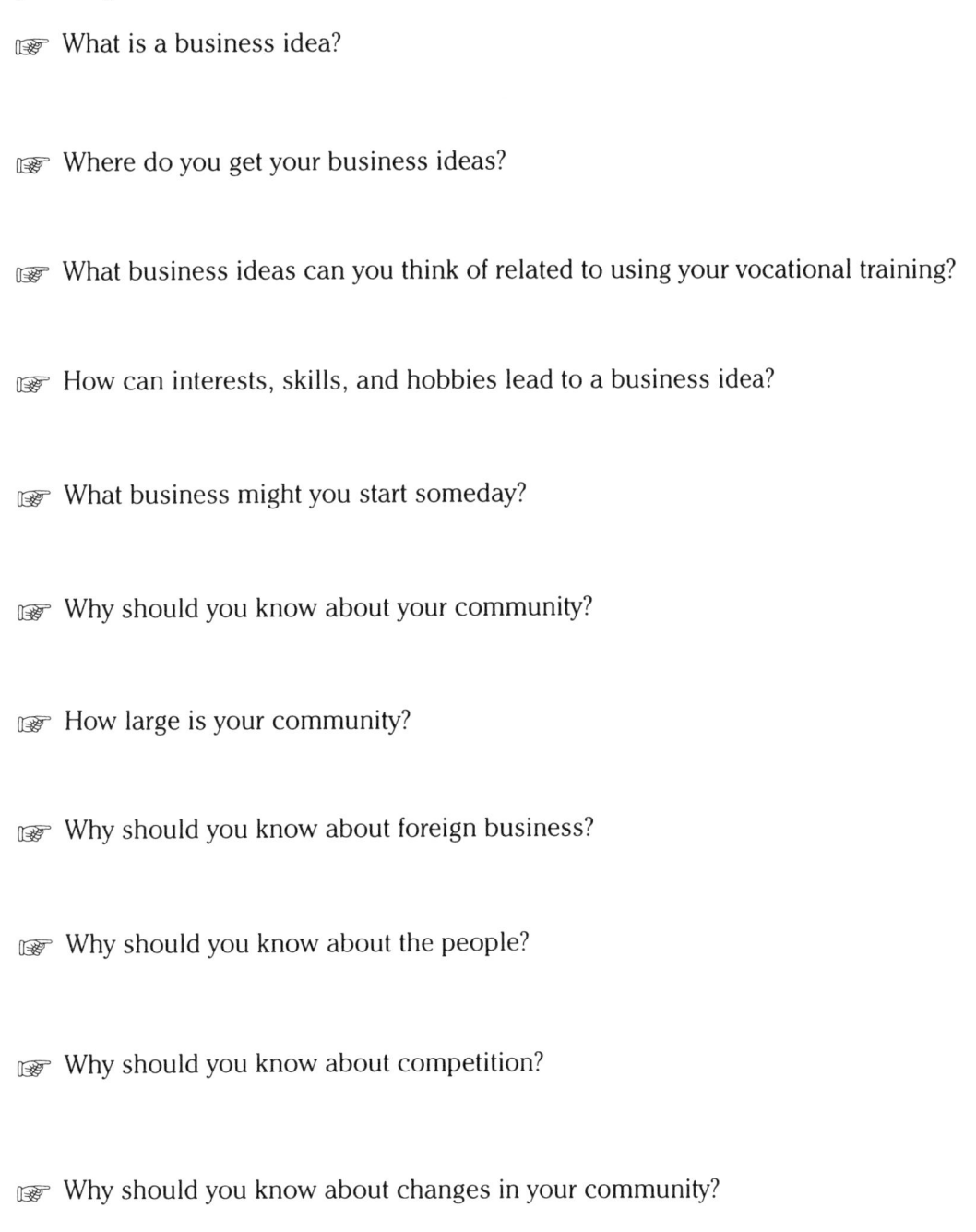

☞ What is a business idea?

☞ Where do you get your business ideas?

☞ What business ideas can you think of related to using your vocational training?

☞ How can interests, skills, and hobbies lead to a business idea?

☞ What business might you start someday?

☞ Why should you know about your community?

☞ How large is your community?

☞ Why should you know about foreign business?

☞ Why should you know about the people?

☞ Why should you know about competition?

☞ Why should you know about changes in your community?

Section 4

How Can I Prepare To Be My Own Boss?

Completing this section will help you—

- ★ view the entrepreneur's approach to risk taking as an "I-can-do-it" attitude

- ★ use decision making effectively

- ★ understand the importance of goal setting

- ★ identify resources you will need to become an entrepreneur

"A turtle only moves ahead by sticking out his neck."

—*Chantal*

What Is This Section About?

Up to this point, you have looked at your personal values and characteristics; the skills you have gained from your experiences, interests, and hobbies; and how you can apply these to a particular business idea.

Maybe you are thinking seriously about the possibility of *being your own boss*. In this unit we will examine the steps you can begin to take that will prepare you to become an entrepreneur some time in your future.

Based on your business idea and the skills and aptitudes that you have, in what skill areas are you weak? You will discover how to develop these "business skills." You will think about the networks of people you meet in the future who may be able to help with your business idea.

The key to unlocking the door to business success is planning. You will have a chance to explore the importance of planning and some strategies for goal setting.

How Do Entrepreneurs View Risk?

When you think of risk, do you conjure up thoughts of gambling, chance, or a blind leap into an unknown situation? These are types of risk, but to the entrepreneur, risk is just another factor to consider in the decision-making process.

If you were to interview entrepreneurs, they would probably say that they did not take a risk when they started their business. They might even tell you that it would have been more of a risk in terms of "lost opportunity" if they had not launched their small business enterprise.

True entrepreneurs approach risk not with the idea that "what can go wrong will go wrong," but with an "I-can-make-it-work-in-my-favor" attitude. They gather information and, based on the facts, make what they feel is a low-risk decision.

Because they view the benefits to be gained from taking a risk and not just the negatives that *might* result, they are able to take advantage of countless opportunities.

Is Becoming an Entrepreneur Too Risky?

In section 2 we talked about experiences—and how we learn from them. Through repetition of activities, we become experts on certain subjects. For example, if you play tennis every day, you may soon become a tennis expert.

The same is true for business. **Working for someone else in a business you want to start may help you become an expert.** Planning for business ownership leads to avoiding problems. Entrepreneurs eliminate much of the risk of starting a business by planning for the future.

Remember, a series of planned experiences leads to a successful future. Whether you learn through planned educational, volunteer, or paid work experiences, becoming an expert reduces the risk of becoming your own boss.

Why Worry about Decisions?

In many aspects of life, and particularly as a small business owner, you are faced with making daily decisions. Some are routine and require little thought. Others are critical and require you to ask questions and think carefully before deciding. Some decisions students may face on an average day include—

Who to ask to the homecoming dance?

What to do Saturday night?

What to wear to school?

When to do homework?

Go on to college or start a career after high school?

As a small business owner, you will continually be faced with making decisions. You will have to make decisions about such things as—

- what merchandise do I add to my inventory?
- what credit plan should I offer customers?
- how do I confront a customer who is shoplifting?
- what will I name my business?

How Do You Make Your Decisions?

We each have a different style of decision making that we use in various situations. Some of these styles are more effective than others. Look at the following strategies:

★ *Impulsive.* Taking the first alternative, with little thought or examination involved.

★ *Fatalistic.* Letting the environment decide; leaving it up to fate—"whatever will be will be."

★ *Compliant.* Letting someone else decide or following someone else's plan—"tell me and I'll do it."

★ *Delaying.* Putting the decision off, postponing thought and action—"I'll cross that bridge later."

★ *Agonizing.* Getting lost in all the data; getting overwhelmed with alternatives; being torn between options.

★ *Planning.* Using the rational procedure to weigh both facts and feelings.

★ *Intuitive.* Doing what feels right; basing the decision on inner harmony.

★ *Paralysis.* Accepting responsibility for the decision, but being unable to approach it—"I just can't face it."

Think of a decision you made today, this week, or this month. Can you identify the style or styles of decision making you used in each of these situations? Was it effective for you? If not, how might you improve your decision-making style or ability?

Personal Profile 13

Career Decision-Making Steps

Career decision-making steps offer a systematic method to evaluate possible career options. Have you ever known a person who just fell into a job and stayed there? He/she may never have realized that there could be another job, or many other jobs, for which they may have been better suited and satisfied. The following steps can prevent this from happening to you. Use these steps to begin to define your career goals.

1. Identify the issue (career choice).

2. Consider the alternatives and collect information on them (get a job at a retail store, entrepreneurship, further education, etc.).

3. Evaluate the alternatives based on your abilities, personal attributes, needs, desires, and goals (need to be in charge, independence, location, etc.)

4. Choose the best alternative.

5. Make a plan to achieve your goal (gain experience in a job, explore funding sources, learn more, build networks, etc.)

6. Prioritize the tasks in your plan and decide how to take action.

7. Decide how to evaluate the results of each task as you move toward your goal.

How Can I Prepare to Be My Own Boss?

Why Are Goals Important?

No matter what you may decide to do with your future, you need to set goals to help you get there. Goals are a road map helping you travel from being a student to becoming an adult employed, for example, as—

- an owner of your own business

- a teacher

- a mechanic

- a homemaker

- a politician

- a salesperson

- a marketing consultant

- a farmer

- a banker

- a secretary

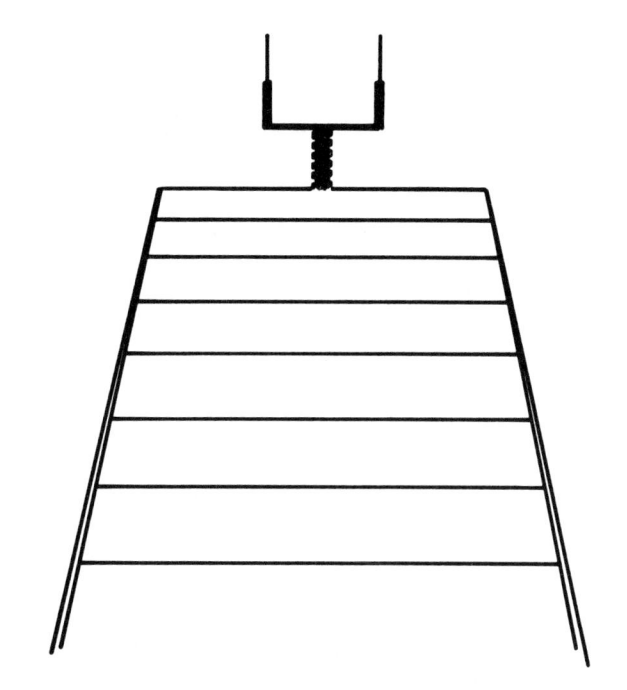

As you begin to plan your future, you need to set *long-term goals* for yourself—goals that you may not reach for 5 to 10 years. Short-term goals are the pit stops that help you reach the end of the race—your long-term goals. For example, John's long-term goal is to own and operate a catering business within 5 years. He may establish the following short-term goals:

- Graduate from high school

- Get a job working for a caterer or restaurant

- Take some business classes from the local community college

- Save extra money

- Obtain a loan

Continued on Next Page

Reaching your short-term goals brings you another step closer to fulfilling your long-term goals. It has been said that if you set goals you know you have accomplished something when you reach them. Otherwise, you may roam aimlessly through life without any direction.

While you prepare for the world of work, think of the jobs you now hold as short-term goals bringing you closer to your long-term goal of a career. A job as a waiter or waitress or host or hostess in a restaurant may begin to prepare you for the many hats that are worn by a restaurant owner.

How Do You Reach Your Goals?

It is not enough to set goals for yourself. You must practice techniques that will enable you to follow through on your goals. How many times have you made New Year's resolutions without any follow-through. Have you failed to—

- lose weight,

- quit smoking, or

- stop being so negative?

Do you lack the motivation to follow through with your goals? The following tips may be helpful in your quest to reach those well-intended promises or goals.

- Set goals based on your personal desires.

- Prioritize your goals and work on the most important ones.

- Keep your goals in view. Write them down and place them where you will constantly see them and be reminded of them. For example, put them—
  —in your wallet,
  —on the refrigerator,
  —in the car,
  —in your locker,
  —on your dresser.

- Imagine yourself fulfilling your goal—actually doing the activity.

- Set time lines for accomplishing your goals.

- Revise your goals as your values, experiences, and needs change.

How Can I Prepare to Be My Own Boss?

Personal Profile 14

Setting Personal Goals

No matter what you may decide to do with your future, you need to set goals to help you get there. This exercise will help you set some short-term and long-term goals for yourself.

Step 1:

The first step in goal setting is to select a long-term goal that you wish to reach and write it here.

My Goal

Step 2:

Short-term goals are the necessary steps toward reaching your long-term goal. In the space, write at least three short-term goals that will help you achieve the long-term goal you identified in step 1.

-
-
-
-
-
-

Continued on Next Page

Step 3:

Prioritize and set time lines for accomplishing your short-term and long-term goals. Number the goals in step 2 in order of priority. Add the date that you plan to complete each step.

Step 4:

Identify what you need to do now to reach your short-term goals within the time lines you have set for yourself. As you develop more goals, both now and in the future, keep this system in mind. If used, it will help you fulfill your goals.

Why Should You Begin to Build Resources?

One short-term goal you can begin to build right now is identifying your resources and planning to make the best possible use of them. **Entrepreneurs use their own expertise and the resources of others to reach their goal of business success**.

We have already talked about the resources we have within ourselves to create a business. You have identified your personal qualifications that help you feel that you can do it. You have looked at the experiences in your life to see the knowledge and skills you already have developed that will help you in a business of your own. And you have used all this information to begin to think of a business you can start someday.

You don't have to depend on yourself alone to start a business. Other people and opportunities for experience are available to anyone who chooses to find them. Your goals should include experiences that make use of all of the resource opportunities in your community. Before you start your business, you need to build a strong foundation of personal resources. Many of these resources will actually supplement the knowledge and skills that you have found you are personally lacking.

Continued on Next Page

What Types of Resources Should You Begin to Build?

Resources for the entrepreneur can include people who provide ideas, help in problem solving, or assist in the business itself. These people will serve as contacts before a business is started and throughout its life.

Resources may also be available in your local library. All kinds of business ideas and ways to solve problems are described by authors who have personal business experience. Up-to-date market data and new product ideas can be found in books, too.

The potential entrepreneur can seek out resources for learning about running a business from courses offered at two-year and four-year colleges and universities. Often, these courses are available to anyone, whether or not he or she is enrolled as a regular student.

A most important resource for the entrepreneur is financing. It is often the hardest resource for the young, inexperienced businessperson to find. Those who have money to invest want to see a credit record that shows you have made wise decisions about your personal finances. For example, buying a car and paying it off as promised help build a good credit record. Your use of your income in the next few years can make a big difference in how banks, seed-capital funds, or friends and relatives respond when you ask for a loan.

Who Are the Contacts?

Resources for the entrepreneur can also include people or contacts who might be a source of information about a particular subject or topic. When building a relationship or establishing communication with contacts, it is important to determine their subject area, knowledge area, or skill. Knowing this can save time when information is needed. Here are some examples of contact people who might be useful in starting a business:

* ***Lawyer.*** This professional can provide you with legal advice, from telling you what sort of ownership you might want to consider, to advising you about government regulations you need to follow.

* ***Accountant.*** This person will help you with financial statements and perhaps advise you on your taxes.

* ***Insurance agent.*** This individual can help minimize your financial loss in case of fire or theft by insuring your business.

- ★ **Shipping agent.** This person will be responsible for the transportation of your products to their proper destination, and also for receiving packages and sending them to the proper place in your business.

- ★ **Sales representative from supplier.** This individual will act as both advisor and salesperson to supply you with products your business will need to operate successfully.

- ★ **Advertising agent.** This professional will ensure that your market knows about your business and what you sell. The advertising agent may advise you on how best to promote and advertise your business.

- ★ **Other businesspeople.** These people may become customers or, while at your place of business, may tell you what your competitor is doing; they may give advice and suggestions.

- ★ **Banker.** This professional can give you financial support (a loan) and advice on cash-related topics.

- ★ **School job placement staff.** These people are in your school to help you find the right job or send you to the right people to give you advice. They are resource people and can help you find the information you need to make career decisions.

- ★ **Current employer.** This important person helps you gain job experience and gives you a paycheck. Also, you might also be able to talk to your employer about your own career plans and ask for advice.

- ★ **Relatives in business.** These people can give you moral support, ideas for career planning, and maybe even experience working for them.

- ★ **Neighbors or friends in business.** Just like your relatives, neighbors and friends can give you a pat on the shoulder, advice on your career plans, and maybe even job experience.

- ★ **Trade associations staff.** These professionals serve as resource contacts for particular trades. They can tell you about new developments in certain areas of business, the education that is available, and who is involved in the trade locally.

- ★ **Vocational teacher.** This important person will teach you new skills, advise you, and prepare you for the world of work.

If you do not possess all necessary talents, your contacts or resources may help lighten the load. Don't hesitate to hire someone to provide technical assistance for your business or to call upon someone who may provide advice for free!

Often success comes from *who* you know as well as *what* you know.

Personal Profile 15

Contact/Resource List

List the names of people you know who might help you acquire additional skills or experience necessary if you start a business. Beside each name list the occupation or title of the person and the experience or expertise they might provide. After completing this worksheet, you will have a good list of sources to contact for beginning your own business.

Name	**Title/Occupation**	**Skill, Experience, Expertise**

What Do You Need to Be Prepared to Do?

Many people go into business without being prepared to do all the jobs required of the boss. Often they fail without even knowing why. When you set goals to prepare yourself for success as an entrepreneur, study the skills of your vocation, learn management techniques, and use all the resources you can along the way—you will reduce the risk and pave the way to success.

Where Can an Entrepreneur Go for Assistance?

Planning is essential for entrepreneurs to be successful in business. Although they often take on what many consider to be a risky situation when starting a business, entrepreneurs plan with an "I-can-do-it" attitude. They set goals for the future to help achieve business success.

Entrepreneurs use their own experiences and the expertise of others to create a successful business. These individuals who provide expertise are entrepreneurs' resources. Potential entrepreneurs should not hesitate to seek the talent and skills they may not yet have. Certainly, entrepreneurs must depend on themselves and the help and advice of others to reach their goals.

Activities

The following activities are planned to help you review the section on "How Can I Prepare to Be My Own Boss?" Also, you will learn more about the process of decision making when you are asked to analyze decisions made in some short cases as well as understand your own choices in making a decision. Read the instructions carefully.

What Is Risk?

Instructions: Risk is different to each person, but generally it means the fear of failure, sticking your neck out, taking a chance, not being sure of yourself. Risk isn't risk when you have the confidence in your ability to do something, and experience builds confidence. List some situations that you once viewed as risky but no longer see that way. Explain why each situation is no longer risky and be prepared to discuss your reasons with the class. Examples may include the following:

- The first day of school
- Trying out for a club or team
- Applying for your first job
- Asking someone for a date
- Speaking in class or in a group
- Water skiing the first time
- Asking someone if they like you

	Situation	**Explanation**
1.		
2.		
3.		
4.		

How Can I Prepare to Be My Own Boss?

Entrepreneurs Wear Many Hats

Instructions: As you start your own business, you will find that you need to know how to do many things. Your experiences in school and on various jobs will help you learn how to do the following. Check the items that you already have at least some experience in.

An Entrepreneur Must Be a(n)

___ Financier	___ Billing Clerk
___ Insurance Manager	___ Stock Clerk
___ Shipper	___ Warehouser
___ Advertising Copywriter	___ Driver
___ Engineer	___ Artist
___ Public Relations Agent	___ Sign Painter
___ Designer	___ Electrician
___ Architect	___ Salesperson
___ Display Artisan	___ Editor
___ Personnel Manager	___ Supervisor
___ Wage Clerk	___ Manager
___ Accountant	___ Superintendent
___ File Clerk	___ Tax Expert
___ Teacher	___ Analyst
___ Bookkeeper	___ Economist
___ Mechanic	___ Inventor
___ Secretary	___ Travel Clerk
___ Groundskeeper	___ Writer
___ Motor Pool Officer	___ Police Officer
___ Showperson	___ Custodian

List goals for your future that will prepare you to wear the many hats of an entrepreneur. My goals are:

1. _____ 4. _____

2. _____ 5. _____

3. _____ 6. _____

How Can I Prepare to Be My Own Boss?

Matching

Instructions: This worksheet will help you review some of the vocabulary from this section. Select the letter of the definition that most clearly fits the term on the left. Write the letter in the space provided.

1. _____ impulsive
2. _____ risk
3. _____ inventory
4. _____ expert
5. _____ self-known desires
6. _____ contacts
7. _____ benefits
8. _____ intuitive
9. _____ short-term goals
10. _____ resources
11. _____ planning
12. _____ career decision
13. _____ agonizing
14. _____ merchandise
15. _____ complaint

a. good things that happen

b. making a choice or coming to a conclusion on career questions

c. a decision-making style described by taking the first alternative with little thought or examination

d. to take a chance with either a good or bad result

e. innermost secret thoughts or dreams

f. the goods that someone wants to sell

g. supply of a product on hand

h. a decision-making style described by letting someone decide for you—"tell me and I'll do it"

i. a person who has high levels of skill or knowledge in a certain area

j. the "pit-stop" results of your efforts that help you to reach long-term goals

k. a decision-making style described by a person using the rational procedure to weigh both facts and feelings

l. people who might be a source of information about a subject or topic

m. a decision-making style described by a person getting lost in all the data, torn between options, or getting overwhelmed with alternatives

n. can be people, books, magazines, or materials that can provide information or advice on certain topics

o. a decision-making style that is described by doing what feels right, or basing a decision on inner harmony

105

How Can I Prepare to Be My Own Boss?

Decision-Making Steps: Word Search

Instructions: This activity will help you learn some of the terms used to describe different decision-making styles. Search the puzzle for the words listed below. The words may appear horizontally, vertically, or diagonally. Circle each word in the puzzle as you find it.

Planning **Paralysis**
Fatalistic **Impulsive**
Delaying **Intuitive**
Compliant **Agonizing**

```
N H C G J O E S S T C I M D L Z
G R H X D Q V I U F W O Z E K Y
W I V F G M S N B U Q N P L X J
H P L A A Y R I D V Y W X V U P
J A L R L X W U F T F G T Q O V
R E S A G Z E S H P A A N U U T
I Q R K N Y F T P L T C R S C R
M A C Y L N G M D A A G T J O Z
P C O M P L I A N T L P A S M F
U O D A A G O N I Z I N G B P A
L D E E G B C A G O S O A N L S
S G A D L O D E V K T N M R Y P
I F P G Z A N M C L I M P U L Q
V K A L W K Y B L P C N L Q G O
E I R H A O M I M P C O X N H F
J N A I G N L I N T U I T I V E
M P L A J O A P B G C M D A E D
```

106

Decision-Making Grid

The decision-making grid will help you to understand your decision clearly and to consider all of your options.

The first item to complete is the problem or question you wish to make a decision on. Fill this in at the top of the grid.

Next, you will see that there are four boxes for you to fill in, the choices among which you must decide. You may need only two of these boxes, or you may need more than are on the grid. Add lines to make more boxes, or use only the number of boxes you need. In the choice boxes, write your choices.

Now you are ready to fill in the input factor boxes. There are 10 spaces for you to write in the input factors or the ingredients to your making a good decision. Now rank these in order of importance, with 10 being the most important factor in your decision and 1 being the least important.

It is time for you to rate your choices against the input factors. This will reflect your own feelings and values and is often difficult to do. Rate your choices from 1 to 10.

Lastly, from having completed the grid, what decision will you make? Write it at the bottom of this page.

Example Grid: This student wanted to make a decision between four types of cars. He or she listed the input factors and the ingredients needed to make the decision, and then rated them from most important to least important. Then she or he rated each factor against the choices as he or she felt each car compared to them. Now, which car do you suppose this student chose from the information on the grid? Discuss this in class before attempting your own grid.

Source: Adapted from Robert Nelson and Allen Mark Perres, *Decision Making*, edited by Edward Nixiol, Cheryl Nelsen, and William Hood (Chicago: Vision Publishing, 1976), pp. 28–45.

SAMPLE GRID

State the Problem/Question: *I want to buy a car which is the best for me.*

Choice 1 Ford Maverick	Choice 2 Chevy Nova	INPUT FACTORS	Choice 3 Plymouth Duster	Choice 4 Volkswagen Beetle
6	5	1. Cost of Car — 9	9	8
5	6	2. Mileage — 10	8	9
7	7	3. Overall Maintenance Cost — 8	6	7
5	4	4. Handling — 6	6	7
7	8	5. Smooth Ride — 9	6	4
7	9	6. Interior Room — 9	7	3
4	4	7. Resale Value — 4	3	6
9	8	8. Easy to Service — 7	5	4
9	9	9. Power — 1	7	3
8	9	10. Styling — 2	9	4

Continued on Next Page

How Can I Prepare to Be My Own Boss?

GRID

Name:

State the Problem/Question:

	Choice 1	Choice 2	INPUT FACTORS	Choice 3	Choice 4
			1.		
			2.		
			3.		
			4.		
			5.		
			6.		
			7.		
			8.		
			9.		
			10.		

Goal Action

Choose one short-term goal developed in Profile 14 and complete one small task today that will be required to accomplish your goal. For example, fill out an application if your goal is to get a job. Write a paragraph about how you felt after doing the task. This should motivate you to move closer to your goal.

Fantasy Autobiography

Instructions: Let's pretend that it is now 10 years in the future. Write an autobiography of how you became a successful entrepreneur. Refer to Success Stories for ideas.

How Can I Prepare to Be My Own Boss?

Success Stories

As you read the following case studies, think about how these entrepreneurs set goals and then worked at reaching them.

Name: Jodee C. Kulp

Business Name: Jodee Kulp Graphic Arts Services

Business Address: 119 North 4th Street, Suite 401
Minneapolis, MN 55401

Business Phone: (612) 341-9870

Type of Business: Full-service graphic arts studio

At age 12 Jodee Kulp had her first experience with business ownership when she and her sister inherited their cousin's earthworm enterprise. Because they had so much competition, Jodee decided their worms had to be special and that packaging would make the difference. She found a source in the colorful packages used by Dairy Queen, used sphagnum moss rather than the usual dirt filler, and learned the secrets of attracting worms to a garden plot. They sold their earthworms to local bait shops and resorts. Says Jodee, "It was a good lesson in business basics."

Jodee's high school program in vocational education was sales and marketing. There she learned accounting, developing free-lance accounts, leadership, and communication skills. Following graduation, she enrolled in Hennepin Technical Center—North Campus, Brooklyn Park, Minnesota—where she completed a two-year course in commercial art. After attending Hennepin Tech she had the opportunity to start a graphic arts firm for a printing company in St. Paul. Her responsibilities included acquiring accounts, invoicing, time management, equipment purchases, and employee management. Jodee feels, "It was an excellent incubation period for developing the basic skills of managing a graphics studio with no financial obligation." She furthered her education with a self-financed year in Sweden, studying graphic arts.

The need to control her own destiny and the need for achievement led Jodee into starting her own business. She was highly creative and hardworking, had management and business operations experience, plus good sales and "people skills." With a $5,000 loan, Jodee opened Graphic Arts Services in her home.

Jodee received help from many sources. She credits family and friends for their support and encouragement, her high school sales and marketing instructor and previous employers for teaching her business and management skills, and her husband who "shared his years of business knowledge and was patient as the business evolved and our lives changed." Her personal accountant offered simple recommendations that she could understand.

Continued on Next Page

Of special importance was her grandfather, who lost his own business during the depression. Jodee says, "He is my strongest mentor.... His wisdom, perceptions and advice have definitely guided me in times of need."

Graphic Arts Services began with Jodee as its only employee, and now has 13 working full time and part time, and a crew of free-lancers. The firm is a sole proprietorship, with gross sales in 1986 of $500,000. Almost all of the profits continue to go back into the business for the purpose of better equipment, employee salaries, and improved working conditions.

From her initial goal of making all her payments to vendors during the first six months, Jodee has expanded. She projects over a million dollars in sales. Jodee believes profits and continued growth go hand in hand. Without profits there is no growth. Says Jodee, "Profits are an integral part of success."

Case Study Questions

Jodee Kulp
Graphics Arts Services

1. Describe the early work and entrepreneurial experiences that encouraged Jodee to start her own business.

2. Jodee had many opportunities to learn business and management skills in high school and vocational school. What were some of these skills?

3. Personal characteristics were as important as artistic skill in Jodee's success. Describe the qualities that made her successful.

4. What were some of the other sources of help and advice that Jodee used when she started her graphics business?

5. In Jodee's view, which is more important, profits or continued growth of her business? What has one to do with the other?

. . . .

Name: Bryan Frick

Business Name: Frick's Place Restaurant

Business Address: 416 East Washington
Pandora, OH 45877

Business Phone: (419) 384-3600

Type of Business: Full-menu, table-service restaurant

Bryan Frick's father worked in a restaurant while Bryan was growing up. Bryan's first interest was in the fancy work of culinary arts: ice carving, chocolate carving, and tallow sculpture.

Bryan chose to major in food service at Apollo Joint Vocational School. His program at Apollo JVS introduced him to entrepreneurship and this got him interested in owning his own business. The program also gave him experience in payroll scheduling, payment of bills, and inventory control.

Upon graduation in 1978, Bryan entered Columbus Technical Institute and graduated in 1981 with an Associate of Applied Business in Hospitality Management Technology degree. The program at Columbus Technical Institute included an apprenticeship component, which gave Bryan supervised, on-the-job experience working in the food industry. Bryan feels this was a real asset. Bryan's experience includes working in a college cafeteria, fancy family restaurant, and a country club. Bryan feels you must not be afraid to work or afraid to start over again.

When Bryan determined he wanted to open his own restaurant, he talked to his former instructors. He also talked with an experienced restaurant operator about business procedures and purchasing techniques. Bryan felt that a family restaurant in Pandora was appropriate since there was no other family restaurant within 30 miles. Bryan knew that his customers would be farmers of Swiss descent and planned his restaurant accordingly. It is a full-menu, table-service restaurant that features all-you-can-eat buffet five days a week.

Financing was a problem in the beginning, since Bryan was only 22. However, Bryan was able to secure a land contract with an option to buy in one year.

Bryan has been in business for three years now. Annual sales last year were worse than projected because the farming economy was down. Seventy-five percent of Bryan's profit goes back into the business. Currently, Bryan employs seven people.

Continued on Next Page

The business has put stress on all family members. In addition to the stress on the family from trying to make the business succeed, it is difficult to find enough time to spend together as a family unit. But Bryan feels you should not be afraid to work—hard.

Even with the stress and lack of family time, Bryan is happy with his decision to go into business for himself. It gives him a feeling of accomplishment as well as a satisfying and reliable income with a potential for increase. Bryan also enjoys being able to use his natural talent for culinary arts and the daily changes and challenges that operating a restaurant and catering parties entail. According to Bryan, "Money is not the whole reason for going into business for myself. I feel the satisfaction of making and serving a meal and making all the customers happy is my main thrill of owning my business."

Just as Bryan set a goal in high school to own his own business, Bryan has set goals for the business. Bryan wants to increase community support, since most of his business is from out-of-towners, and to maintain a quality restaurant. Bryan plans to achieve his goals through hard work, continuous education, and community involvement.

Bryan felt he would achieve long-term success when business was better than anticipated during his first month. Bryan will feel successful, however, when everything runs smoothly not only when he's there, but also when he's away.

Bryan is a Certified Working Chef, a designation he worked hard to achieve. In addition, he is a member of the Apollo Career Center Advisory Committee for Food Service, Pandora Jaycees, Pandora Business Association, Columbus Chef's Association, National Restaurant Association, and a consultant for Ohio State Department of Vocational Home Economics. His most recent award was second place for individual pastry display at the Columbus Chef's Culinary Salon, an American Culinary Federation-approved show in 1985. Other awards include second place for bread display at the American Culinary Federation (ACF)-approved show in Cincinnati, first and second place awards for bread and tallow display at an ACF-approved show in Louisville, Kentucky, third place in the Apprenticeship Student Category at an ACF-approved show in Dayton, and first place at a Chef Showcase at the Ohio FHA/HERO Recognition Activity.

Case Study Questions

Bryan Frick
Frick's Place Restaurant

1. What elements in Bryan's life do you feel were instrumental in helping him decide to become an entrepreneur (hint: skills, interests, hobbies)?

2. Why do you feel Bryan is a planner?

3. Identify the major resource persons with whom Bryan spoke about starting his own business.

4. What did Bryan know about his customers?

5. How did information about his customers help Bryan decide what sort of restaurant would succeed?

6. Describe Bryan's goals for his business.

Name: Raul Avila

Business Name: Avila and Co.

Business Address: 1255 Corporate Center Drive, Suite 202
Monterey Park, CA 91754

Business Phone: (213) 262-1201

Type of Business: Real-estate investment

Raul Avila credits his family with much of the success of his seven-year-old real estate investment business. His father had started his own electrical contracting business years earlier when he moved to Los Angeles from El Paso and found that no one would give him a job. Now a successful businessman, he provided financial support for Raul's venture, as well as an example of successful entrepreneurship.

Raul actually got the idea for starting his company when he worked in his oldest brother's real estate management company. Raul's sister worked for him there as secretary and bookkeeper and is presently employed by Avila and Co. as his property supervisor.

But there were other circumstances besides family that led Raul to start his own business. A highly motivated student, he attended Catholic parochial schools where he learned excellent communication skills as well as self-discipline. Playing in the school band taught him coordination and teamwork. He studied business administration and building technology at Don Bosco Technical Institute, Rosemead, California, where he excelled at architectural design.

Community service is an important part of Raul's personal make-up and of his life. He observed very early that no business succeeds unless it provides a service to the community. He also saw that his community needed opportunities to expand, and that locally there were many property owners who were tired of managing their rental property but who wanted to continue to own real estate. He saw the profitability of buying and selling income-distressed property.

These observations, together with Raul's education, self-discipline, motivation, and community spirit, helped determine the type of business he would choose. The risks were "frightening," Raul says. Real estate development requires significant amounts of start-up capital for publicity, marketing, and promotion to investors. A $15,000 loan from Bank of America helped him begin.

Annual sales are now in the $600,000 range, and Raul projects that they may reach $3 million in two years. He puts almost all profits back into the Avila and Co. and is in the process of incorporating the business, which was formerly a partnership.

Because of his training in both business administration and building technology, Raul is able to provide all services for every property he purchases: negotiating, insurance, financing, construction, management, and sales.

Real estate development provides a base for the community service that is important to Raul. Although he was only 20 years old when he started in business ("It was difficult many times for bankers and brokers to take me seriously," he says), Raul was elected president of the local Rotary Club at age 24. He serves as a city commissioner for Monterey Park, a field representative for a U.S. Congressman, a police reserve officer, and is on the boards of several community organizations.

He views his business as a means to serve a wide spectrum of people, from first-time home buyers to seasoned investors. He believes that in every business setback is the seed of a new opportunity. He is excited by the limitless opportunities in his chosen field. "I am my only limitation," Raul says.

Case Study Questions

Raul Avila
Real estate investment

1. What kind of personal characteristics does Raul believe have helped to contribute to his business success?

2. How did Raul's father and brother help him in making a decision to start a small business?

3. What did Raul know about the needs of the community that made his business different from his competitors?

4. What kinds of education experiences contributed to Raul's ability to go into business for himself?

5. How has Raul's community interests influenced both his goals he has set for his company and how he spends his spare time?

The Think Tank

How Can I Prepare to Be My Own Boss?

Instructions: Summarize what you have learned in this section by answering the following questions. Keep this as a private journal entry to use in your future career planning.

☞ How do entrepreneurs view risk?

☞ Is becoming an entrepreneur too risky?

☞ Why worry about decisions?

☞ How do you make your decisions?

☞ Why are goals important?

☞ How do you reach your goals?

☞ Why should you begin to build resources?

☞ What types of resources should you begin to build?

☞ Who are the contacts?

☞ What do you need to be prepared to do?

Glossary

aptitude	a natural talent or inclination for certain activities
assessment	the determination of the amount of entrepreneurial characteristics that you possess
average per-capita income	average earnings of persons in your market area
average per-family income	average earnings of families in your market area
benefits	to receive advantages or good things
business planner	a professional who systematically manages the tasks of the business to achieve success
career decision	making a choice about the profession you want to pursue
career options	lifework choices
competition	the efforts of two or more businesses to secure the consumer's business
contacts	individuals who might be a source of information about a subject or topic helpful to your business
corporation	chartered by the state, this business operates as a legal entity separate from its owners
creative ideas	new or novel thoughts
creativity	the ability to make or bring into existence something new
credentials	having adequate skills in a particular profession
credo	a set of beliefs
demographics	statistical characteristics of populations such as age, income, sex, etc.
enthusiasm	strong feelings of excitement
entrepreneur	one who organizes, manages, and assumes the risks of a business
entrepreneurship	assuming the risks of owning your own business
experience	knowledge or skills acquired through watching or being involved in an event

expert	a person who has high levels of skill in a certain area
expertise	high level of skill or knowledge in a specific area
export	selling our country's products to other nations
hobby	an activity that someone does in his or her spare time because it is enjoyable and relaxing
human resources	the people employed by a business
import	buying products from other countries
import substitution	producing goods in our country to replace goods being imported from other countries
interests	subjects that you like to read, hear about, or be involved with
inventory	a supply of a product
investment	the use of money to produce income or profit
knowledge	understanding of a subject gained through experience, or learning and study
leisure	time free from work or duties
leisure activities	ways one spends time away from work or duties
life-style	ways in which people live and spend time and money
long-term goals	the end results of your efforts in a career, which you may not reach for 5 or even 10 years
market	a specified category of potential buyers
market area	a specified geographic area of potential buyers
merchandise	the goods that someone wants to sell
new technologies	updated scientific methods of achieving practical purposes
partnership	legal organization of a business with more than one person owning-managing the business
resources	people, books, magazines, or materials that can provide information or advice on certain topics
rewards	something given for a service done or provided
risk	to take a chance with either good or bad results

self-known desires	innermost or secret thoughts or dreams
short-term goals	the pit-stop results of your efforts that help you reach long-term goals
skill	successful application of knowledge acquired; demonstration of this application is running a business
sole proprietorship	legal organization of a business with a single owner
values	the beliefs, activities, and so forth, that one prizes or rates highly
venture	a business undertaking involving a chance or risk

Entrepreneur's Response Key for Personal Profile 1B

The answers you see here are what studies have shown to be the common responses given by entrepreneurs. Compare your answers to these responses. To gain the maximum benefit from this exercise, note the personal characteristics indicated in parentheses.

		Rarely or No	Mostly or Yes
1.	Do you like taking chances? (risk taking)		X
2.	Do you like school? (learning oriented)		X
3.	Do you like making your own decisions on the job? (independence, responsibility)		X
4.	Do you get bored easily? (impatience, energy)		X
5.	Do you sleep as little as possible? (energy, time management)		X
6.	Do you feel unexpected energy when you tackle things that you like? (energy, resourcefulness)		X
7.	Do you finish what you start? (determination)		X
8.	Do you take risks for the adventure of it? (risk taking)		X
9.	Do you plan your tasks before getting started? (goal setting, management)		X
10.	Do you worry about what others think of you? (self-confidence)	X	
11.	Do you find it easy to get others to do something for you? (leadership)		X
12.	Do you enjoy doing something just to prove you can do it? (need to achieve)		X
13.	Do you find yourself constantly thinking up new ideas? (creativity)		X
14.	Do you like to take care of details? (impatience)	X	
15.	Do you believe there should be security in a job? (self-confidence)	X	